Praise for
Partnerships Reimagined

I loved this book! Linda and Sharon really dove deep into everything you need to know about corporate partnerships. It's like they read the minds of partnership pros, answering all their burning questions. This is the go-to guide for any non-profit looking to step up their game and bring in more corporate support. In my book, this book is five stars!

Joe Waters, Selfish Giving USA

Are you keen to team up with companies to make a bigger impact? This easy-to-digest book is your go-to-whoa roadmap. It's an empowering read that reminds you of what's important and gives an easy-to-apply strategic checklist for your non-profit. My favourite bits? How to become partner-ready, engaging internal stakeholders, avoiding the cycle of frustration, reading corporate websites differently, idea-sparking stories of powerful partnerships, memorable acronyms so you retain the principles and pithy phrases that force you to do better, like 'solve, don't sell'. My advice? Take a couple of days out. Read each chapter, diagnose where to lift your game and populate your own improved partnership strategy and implementation plan.

Dr Wendy Scaife, Adjunct Associate Professor, Australian Centre for Philanthropy and Non-profit Studies, Queensland University of Technology (QUT)

Partnerships Reimagined is a must-read for anyone interested in gaining support to create impact. It highlights that these are unique relationships and provides a roadmap to success and avoiding barriers.

John McLeod, Senior Consultant, JBWere

There is so much valuable information in this book. Linda and Sharon really embrace one of the best things about the not-for-profit sector: honest knowledge sharing buoyed by a genuine desire for everyone to succeed in the quest to make the world a better place. Such wisdom in practical, relevant and intelligent advice sets future and current corporate partnership managers on a path to success.

It all resonated. I found myself nodding in agreement as I read, smiling at their humour and wishing I'd had this book when I started off in the world of corporate partnerships.

If you are already working in this space, it will inspire you to do more. It may reassure your current decisions and will most certainly challenge how you think about corporate partnerships. The real-life examples of successful partnerships are great for not-for-profits to think outside the box, as the book looks to break with tradition and move with the times.

If you are new to corporate partnerships, the book is laden with insightful tips that your charity can use to develop a solid strategy. It offers a blueprint for achieving your ultimate corporate partnership. If you use all the tips and follow the advice which can be found in the many templates, diagrams and examples, you will be on your way to landing your next sustainable and significant corporate partnership.

The Find, Win, Grow model is easy to adapt to your current partnership plan or to follow when you are at a loss for where to start. Corporate philanthropy has evolved, and this book will help you to learn, grow and move with those changes. But most importantly, it will help you succeed!

Sally Sweeney, Head of Dolly's Dream

Partnerships Reimagined offers an insightful exploration into the intricacies of cultivating corporate partnerships. The book effectively underscores the necessity for NFPs to undergo internal readiness assessments across all departments before engaging in partnerships, emphasising the importance of aligning organisational capabilities with partnership deliverables.

The Find, Win, Grow approach provides a clear roadmap for cultivating sustainable and impactful relationships with corporate partners. Research is pivotal in understanding their business objectives and tailoring proposals to align with their interests while staying true to your NFP values.

Building relationships and effective communications within the whole organisation are key to ensuring the longevity and success of a partnership. Overall, *Partnerships Reimagined* serves as an invaluable resource for NFPs seeking to navigate the complexities of corporate partnerships, offering practical insights and actionable strategies for fostering collaborative relationships that drive collective impact.

Lisa Woolf-Jones, Chief Xperience Officer,
Kids with Cancer Foundation

This is the book the NFP sector needs. For too long, corporate partnerships have been a source of frustration and mystery, with untapped potential. At last, we have a roadmap and clarity on the way forward. *Partnerships Reimagined* provides practical tips and tools along with plenty of inspiration to help charities raise their game. It's a perfect resource for smaller charities that have no training budget. It's also invaluable for bigger NFPs that want to take their partnerships to the next level. Board directors and CEOs should read it and reshape their approach to partnerships. Those at the coalface will finally have a guide for bigger, more valuable and impactful corporate partnerships.

I have long admired Linda and Sharon and the rigour they bring to the sector. Few people in the southern hemisphere understand corporate partnerships better. So, this book will be invaluable for our sector to get the right advice from those who advise and build partnerships every day.

Julia Keady, CEO, Benefolk

As a non-profit fundraising to help fill the gaps facing children, Variety – the Children's Charity has benefitted from the strategies outlined in *Partnerships Reimagined*. This book steps out a tried and tested process to engage corporate organisations in productive, collaborative and durable partnerships.

Helpfully, authors (and corporate community partnership experts) Linda and Sharon use their extensive experience and success to support non-profits to lay strong partnership foundations. Variety has benefitted through FINDing prospective corporate partners with strong alignment. We are primed to WIN corporate partners to help us do more to reduce the challenges facing children living with disability and disadvantage.

Mandy Burns, CEO, Variety

Partnerships Reimagined

PARTNERSHIPS REIMAGINED

NON-PROFIT STRATEGIES TO CAPTURE CORPORATE VALUE

LINDA GARNETT & SHARON DANN

Published by Stellar Partnerships

First published in 2024 in Melbourne, Australia

Copyright © Linda Garnett & Sharon Dann

www.stellarpartnerships.com

The moral rights of the authors have been asserted.

Edited by Jenny Magee

Typeset and printed in Australia by BookPOD

ISBN: 978-0-9756443-0-0 (paperback)

ISBN: 978-0-9756443-1-7 (ebook)

NATIONAL LIBRARY OF AUSTRALIA

A catalogue record for this book is available from the National Library of Australia

Contents

Introduction   1

Letter to the reader   2
Letter to our younger selves   3
Busting the common myths about partnerships   7
How to use this book   10

1: The Changing Landscape of Partnerships   15

The evolution of corporate partnerships   17
The impact of COVID-19 and the cost-of-living crisis   22
The spectrum of corporate approaches to partnerships   24
Typical responses from non-profits   28
Corporates need you to be the solution   32
Conclusion   36

2 The Opportunity for Non-profits   37

The size of the opportunity is growing   37
Taking the F-word out of partnerships   40
Getting the full value of partnerships   42
Partnerships as an ecosystem   47
Harnessing the opportunity   49
Conclusion   54

3 FIND New Partners   55

FOCUS   58
IDENTIFY   62
NAVIGATE   65
DECIDE   68
Partnerships require a proactive approach   73
Conclusion   77

4 WIN New Partners   79

The secret ingredient for success   81
Shaking off old habits   83
Preparation and research   86
Best sources of information   88
Developing your partnership hypothesis   92
Getting the first meeting   94
At the first meeting   99
The discovery meeting   100
The 5Ps of pitching and proposals   104
Pricing and how much to ask for   108
Dealing with objections   111
Conclusion   115

5 GROW Exceptional Partners   117

Prioritise   118
Nurture   122
Maximise value   128
Making a graceful exit   130
Conclusion   138

6 It Takes a Village   139

Partnerships present unique challenges   140
The role of leadership   144
Recruit for success   147
Mobilise your colleagues   150
Internal stakeholder checklist   150
The particular challenges of a federated organisation   155
Overcoming organisational boundaries   159
The costs and benefits of mobilising your village   161
Conclusion   163

7 Hello from the Other Side   165

Understanding your corporate audience   169
What's keeping corporate CEOs awake at night?   170
The payoff for getting it right   173
You have more in common than you realise   174
Solve, don't sell   178
Common themes and trends in partnerships   179
The best questions to ask each other   182
Conclusion   185

Afterword   187

Work with us   191

About the Authors   193

References   197

Acknowledgments   203

Want More?   205

Introduction

Corporate partnership (definition): a mutually beneficial relationship between a for-profit company and a non-profit organisation.

Corporate partnerships are the least understood area in any non-profit. For too long, they've been seen as marginal, too hard or not worth the effort. This book aims to change your view of corporate partnerships and inspire you with the potential for your organisation. It contains a mixture of practical and useful tools, research on trends and case studies and examples. Most of all, it distils years of experience from authors who have walked your path and learned the hard way.

Linda Garnett spent decades in the corporate sector working in finance and strategy. Like many people seeking purpose and fulfilment, she switched direction to work with and within non-profit organisations. How hard could it be to apply those corporate skills to solving societal problems? It turned out to be a lot harder than she expected. The cultural differences were enormous and there was no obvious roadmap to success.

Sharon Dann has worked in fundraising forever. She started as an enterprising face-to-face fundraiser, getting people to part with their credit card details within five minutes of the first smile. Her natural sales skills were a big advantage for partnerships, but frustratingly, the usual fundraising approaches didn't work. There was no-one to turn to for guidance.

We've written this book for everyone who wants to realise the potential of corporate partnerships, no matter where your career started. We get you because we've been you. This is the book we wished we had at the beginning.

Letter to the reader

Working in partnerships can be lonely. Your colleagues don't understand what you do and your boss certainly doesn't get it. But you know you've got fabulous skills and experiences that can make the world a better place. You just need a structured pathway and a little help to unlock all that potential.

You've made sacrifices to be here. You could be earning a fat salary on the corporate side and be sipping cocktails at the latest corporate strategy away day. You could also be bored out of your brain and despairing at the utter pointlessness of your role. Yet another 20-person stakeholder committee to sell a product that no one needs or rework a document that nobody will read.

You made the right decision to jump into partnerships. If we're going to fix the big, gnarly problems in the world, we need everyone to lean in. Once you see the potential you could achieve by bringing together the combined expertise, networks, resources and ambition of the corporate and non-profit sectors you'll be hungry for more.

Partnerships are the most fun place to be. You get to be creative, resourceful, savvy and adaptable. You'll build skills you never thought you could have and the confidence to mix it with everyone from CEOs down.

We wrote this book to help you along the journey. When you first embark on corporate-community partnerships, it can feel like being in a foreign country without the language or a guidebook.

This is the book you need. It will help you avoid the pitfalls and traps that get you stuck in a cycle of frustration. It will help you navigate a clear path to the riches at the end of the partnership rainbow. It will help you bring your leadership and your colleagues on the path with you. Most of all, you'll feel someone gets you and your challenges. You'll be supported along the whole journey.

Don't let anyone tell you it's too hard, too slow or too marginal. The world has shifted, and the partnership planets are in alignment right now. Get going and get started, for today is your day. As Dr Seuss said, 'Your mountain is waiting, so get on your way!'

Letter to our younger selves

When we reflect on our years working in corporate partnerships, there are certain things we wish we'd known at the start that would have made life easier. Only in the rear-view mirror can you realise how far you've come.

Here's what we'd say to our younger selves.

Dear Newbie,

Congratulations on leaving the bullsh*t corporate job that sucked your soul dry. You've chosen to make a difference instead. Unfortunately, that difference will show up instantly in your wage packet, so embrace salary packaging with gusto and hoard those meal receipts.

Your mum thinks you're saving the world, and former colleagues look upon you with envy as they attend their umpteenth compliance training away day. Bask in the glow of righteousness for a little while. You'll find working for non-profits is 50% inspiration and 50% frustration, although not always in that order.

There is no shortage of passion for the cause, unlike your previous job where HR posts the corporate values on the wall because no one remembers what the company stands for. Sometimes that passion can stymie real decision-making, as everyone has strong views. There isn't an easy objective measure for choosing between clean water, children's education or a cure for cancer, so there's plenty of spirited argument.

You speak a different language, coming from the corporate world. Everyone has acronyms, but you've never seen so many in one place. Start a glossary and learn how to talk non-profit language. Spend time learning about your programs or meeting the people you're helping. It might even win over that program guy with the dreadlocks and Save the Whales T-shirt who looks at you like you've dropped in from outer space. Which reminds me, the dress code is different. Sharp grey suits are out. Learn to embrace scarves — preferably organic, ethically sourced ones made by the empowered female weaving collective you're busy lifting out of poverty.

In corporate land, you're used to suppliers competing for your attention. You commanded market power and they flocked to you. On the non-profit side of the fence, you're one of thousands trying to get corporate attention. You don't have products to offer; you're selling hope. You need to use your corporate knowledge to solve their problems and make yourself relevant. Otherwise, you'll be shouting about your wonderful cause and getting drowned in the sea of similar non-profit voices.

You can't do corporate partnerships alone. You may be the only one with the big revenue KPI, but it takes the whole organisation to support you. Unfortunately, your colleagues haven't realised this yet. You'll need to convert them to allies and supporters. Show up at team presentations, give them regular bulletins and encourage them to participate. Most of all, get to your board. You will need their networks and leadership support to be successful in partnerships.

Corporate partnerships will allow you to unleash every bit of talent, creativity, skill and experience you've gathered so far. Corporate life puts you in a box and forces you to specialise so narrowly that you only use a fraction of your talent. Partnerships throw open the doors and let you roam across a universe of potential. You'll deal with all sorts on the corporate side: marketing, HR, sales, CSR managers and CEOs. You won't become an expert in everything, but you'll be learning fast.

At times, it will feel like you're wading through treacle. Corporate partners are slow to respond or are doing their fifth restructure that year. Your colleagues have forgotten to tell you that the impact report will be two months late. Your income KPI seems like a mountain to climb. But never doubt that you're in the best possible place — despite the frustrations. You're the one who will change the world for good. You'll tap into the strengths and assets of your corporate partners and help good people make a real difference to society. And your mum will be extra proud.

Yours sincerely,

Your Future Self

Busting the common myths about partnerships

History books are full of false things we once thought true. For centuries, people believed the earth was flat and that sea dragons lived beyond the outer edge. It wasn't a great incentive for sailors, who baulked at exploring too far in case they fell off the edge into the dreaded abyss. In 2023, there is still a diehard Flat Earth Society that is part of a new anti-science movement, but the majority view has moved on. Still, the T-shirts are favourites with cheekily ironic science students.

Holding fast to myths or beliefs can hold you back as much as mindless positivity. The author, Chris Helder, advocates for useful beliefs that help you deal with your current challenges and create an action plan to take you where you want to be.[1]

You can reframe common partnership myths and turn them into useful actions.

We're too small

It's easy to get partnership envy when you see big non-profit brands win multi-million-dollar partnerships. You think that partnerships aren't possible for your small, grassroots organisation. But size isn't always an asset. Sometimes, corporates think the big brands don't need their help as they've got plenty of other options. Size is less important than clarity on your value proposition and what you need from a partner.

During the devastating 2020 Australian bushfires, the Goongerah Wombat Orphanage struggled to rescue injured wildlife. Their partnership with RACV Solar enabled them to upgrade their entire operation and keep baby wombats warm and safe. A wonderful example of a volunteer led, grassroots organisation knowing exactly what it needed and finding the perfect partner.

We're not national

Not every corporate wants a national partner. If you're state-based only or have a small footprint, you probably have strong relationships with local communities and a deep connection to their needs and challenges. When the Sydney Film Festival wanted new partners, they looked for businesses that matched their values and footprint. The partnership with Mountain Goat Beer was a great fit because the brewery had already supported other arts events and was looking to extend operations into Sydney. It's not helpful to focus on what you don't have and limit your options. Focus on the depth of knowledge, credibility and connections within your location and you'll have a strong proposition for the partners who want that alignment.

My board has no corporate contacts

Your board may not have a magic address book to offer you hot prospects. But maybe their connections aren't right for your organisation. Be clear on your organisational needs, your strategic priorities, what you can offer and what will help you achieve your mission. That's where the board adds value for you, especially if they're willing to speak for your non-profit and support partnership prospecting. If your board had the private mobile numbers of every ASX-listed CEO, what would you do if you couldn't answer these fundamental questions?

I just need to get out there

Out where, exactly? For partnership executives and their bosses who've had sales experience, it's a common mantra. There's an expectation that more sales calls equate to more partnerships. Whilst it's true that few partnerships have been won by just waiting for the phone to ring, focusing on the volume of activity can lead you down a blind alley. Without a plan, you're just a tourist with random experiences. It's far more useful to define your destination and then figure out which corporates can help you get there. The willingness to go prospecting for partners is great, but it's effective to first figure out where you want to go.

Partnerships are too hard

Everything looks hard when you haven't tried it yet. It's scary when you're exploring new territory without a map, a guide or a translator. Linda once got lost in the subway in Tokyo, as she could not read Japanese characters. Asking for help and some creative sign language finally found the destination. On the other side of risk is opportunity, so don't be afraid to take some risks and venture into the unknown.

Myths and unhelpful beliefs can hold you back when you embark on corporate partnerships. Some of them are not even beliefs but procrastination borne of fear. Don't use the common myths as an excuse for progress; reframe them as challenges that can be overcome with a different approach. The opportunity is waiting.

How to use this book

Corporate partnerships can't be distilled into one book. They are a universe of possibilities, each unique and challenging in its own way.

This book is intended as a guide for non-profits starting out in corporate partnerships. It will give you the foundational elements and set you up for future success. We want you to avoid the pitfalls, mistakes and trials that we experienced. Every non-profit has the potential for partnership success; you just need a roadmap to get there.

The first step is to understand what's changed in the landscape. What makes *now* the best time to embark on partnerships? Chapters One and Two will challenge what you thought you knew about partnerships and open your eyes to a new perspective. The opportunity is immense, but getting to that opportunity can be daunting. Where and how to get started if you're new to partnerships? How do you get your partnerships back on track if you've started and got stuck?

Chapters Three, Four and Five outline a simple, detailed and logical process to get you from a standing start to confidently securing new and valuable partners. You'll find easy-to-use tools, techniques and templates that you can immediately put into practice. You'll have all the key elements to adapt and modify for your organisation and your personal style. Importantly, you'll have a methodology that you can replicate time and time again and teach to the rest of your team. You'll be able to use a common language and a consistent approach as you grow.

The process has three key elements.

FIND guides you through the internal analysis and reflection that is crucial before you pick up the phone to speak to a prospective corporate partner. It provides the strategic foundation for your partnerships and ensure that partners clearly help deliver on your mission and goals.

WIN provides the tools, methodology and templates to help you make effective external connections with corporates.

GROW builds on your hard work in partnership acquisition and ensures that your partnerships can evolve into a mutual collaboration of sustainable value for both of you.

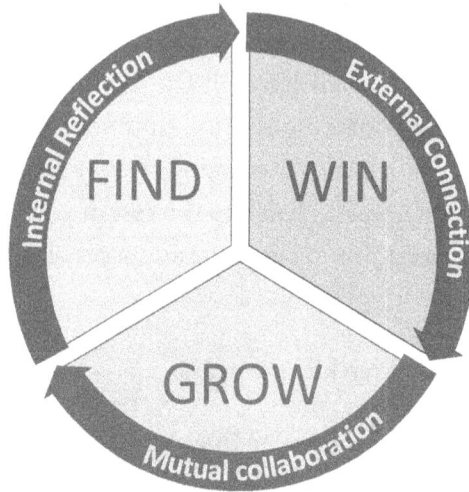

Figure 1: FIND, WIN, GROW model

The final chapters offer insights into what else it will take to be successful. These are the hidden elements that trip up the most seasoned organisations.

Chapter Six addresses one of the greatest barriers to success for people working on partnerships: the need for internal support within your organisation. You've likely encountered some of these challenges already. There may be no one in your organisation with experience of partnerships, or perhaps you're responding to requests that throw you off track. If you want key organisational stakeholders to support you, get them to read Chapter Six.

And finally, Chapter Seven reminds you of the principle underpinning corporate partnerships. It's not about you; it's about them. Perspective and the search for mutual value are the things that differentiate partnerships from fundraising or philanthropy. Embracing this principle can be the hardest thing for non-profits driven by the constant pressure for survival. The more you sharpen your understanding, empathy, curiosity and perspective, the more successful you will be in partnerships.

The process will enable non-profits to build deeper relationships, offer a more compelling proposition for corporate partners and unlock the full value of working with the corporate sector.

We've made partnerships our mission so that you can achieve yours. If you want to get going, get started.

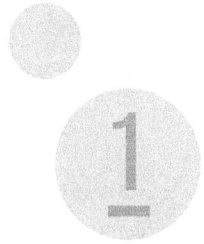

The Changing Landscape of Partnerships

There are many ways to land a plane, as Linda learned when training for her private pilot's licence.

One memorable method is called a controlled descent into terrain. This happens when a pilot is fixated on the dashboard, checking readings and second-guessing them until the plane crashes. There's nothing technically wrong with the plane. The pilot is in full control, but they lack awareness of the looming disaster until it's too late. They need to lift their head above the dashboard and check the horizon to realise the ground is dangerously close.

History is full of organisations that failed to get their heads out of the cockpit and read the situation around them. That's why we no longer rent videos from Blockbuster, use Kodak film for our pictures or connect on Blackberry phones.

COVID-19 caused a seismic shift in society and changed the landscape of corporate-community partnerships forever. But corporate partnerships have been evolving over decades, so the pandemic simply accelerated underlying trends.

To some non-profits, corporate partnerships are a mythical unicorn. These organisations see the incredible things others achieve with their corporate partners, so their boards want corporate partnerships programs too. Or they might have given it a try but haven't made any progress.

This book will help you make friends with corporate partnerships unicorns and unleash the magic for your cause.

You don't need to be the biggest charity with the sexiest cause to be successful at corporate partnerships. You don't need a database of hundreds of thousands of supporters to run an amazing marketing campaign with a partner. You also don't have to create endless group volunteering activities.

What you do need is to think differently about partnerships. A partnership revolution is underway, and non-profits must adapt quickly to survive and thrive. The prize is getting larger and more valuable for those who have already adapted. If you want a slice of what they're having, you'll need to shed old ways of thinking and harness that unicorn.

The evolution of corporate partnerships

The first step to embracing corporate-community partnerships is to get your head out of the cockpit and understand what's changed in the environment.

Corporate philanthropy

Giving has been around since biblical times when Moses asked for contributions towards temple building. Corporate philanthropy, in the form of a charitable donation, is a tax-deductible transaction. The corporate gives to a charity to buy community goodwill and positive PR, or perhaps there is a personal connection to a cause within the business leadership. Corporate philanthropy has not completely disappeared and is always a welcome addition to a non-profit's bottom line. However, there are some serious limitations for non-profits relying on corporate philanthropy.

Typically, a corporate wants to give to a particular program or service. That means restrictions on how the non-profit can allocate the funds. It's also likely that the non-profit is expected to keep overheads low, so the corporate can claim maximum reach and impact for their gift. If they're lucky, non-profits can add 10-15% on top of program costs, which often means they dip into their reserves to fully implement what is needed.

The other problem is the size of the philanthropic donation. Corporates and businesses of all sizes are accountable to their stakeholders, whether they are shareholders, investors or business owners. For 50 years, the prevailing mentality has been the Milton Friedman doctrine that business exists only to create profit.[1] Whilst that may be changing in the 21st century, the legacy remains that philanthropy is a tiny budget item in the bigger plan; a cheap investment to buy goodwill. It's like turning up to a potluck dinner with a bag of Doritos. The corporates are making a token contribution to reap the benefits that others have created.

> Corporate philanthropy is an unreliable source if your non-profit wants sustainable, predictable, long-term income and support.

Corporate philanthropy isn't a true partnership. It's simply a series of one-night stands that give short-term satisfaction. Given the hidden costs of implementing everything a corporate may want in return, a non-profit can find that the one-night stand creates more problems than it was worth. It won't necessarily translate to a longer-term relationship. Once the implementation is done, the corporate is highly likely to move onto the next exciting story for its PR machine. Corporate philanthropy is an unreliable source if your non-profit wants sustainable, predictable, long-term income and support.

Sponsorships

Commercial sponsorships are big business, requiring an exchange of money for very specific outcomes, such as TV rights, access to audiences and brand activations. You can see it any time you watch a sporting event. Sponsorship is often used interchangeably with the word partnership, but a non-commercial sponsorship is really corporate philanthropy in a smarter suit. Your non-profit may have a corporate sponsor for your gala ball, fun run or charity bike ride. The sponsor may want some PR or marketing at the event, but the value to the corporate isn't the same as five billion viewers at the Olympics opening ceremony. It's largely about goodwill, PR content and access to your audiences.

The risk for your non-profit is that non-commercial sponsorship is declining. The 2018 *Support Report* by wealth managers JBWere indicated that large businesses are far more likely to enter into partnerships with for-purpose organisations than simply writing a cheque or entering into a non-commercial sponsorship.[2] The report predicted a significant growth in corporate partnerships by 2036, far outstripping a modest increase in sponsorships.

In 2023, corporates are looking for deeper relationships, greater alignment to their business, staff engagement opportunities and a broader view of value beyond cash. Even in the arts and culture sector, where sponsorship has been the mainstay of operations for many years, corporates are looking for more than logos on programs and free tickets. They seek ways to leverage their core skills, values and strengths to significantly impact society. If your non-profit is still relying on the traditional 'case for support' philanthropy or non-commercial sponsorship for events, then your income base is at risk.

Cause-related marketing and campaigns

Cause-related marketing is a collaborative effort between businesses and non-profits for mutual benefit. It is not tax deductible like corporate philanthropy, as it involves both commercial benefit for the business and a positive impact for a charitable cause. Cause-related marketing has been reaching the mass market since the early 1980s and became highly visible during the Pink Ribbon initiatives to raise money for breast cancer.

Whilst there is still a place for cause-related marketing in the partnership mix, it's no longer an easy cash cow. Consumers are increasingly sceptical of how much money actually reaches the related charity and whether the corporate brand is truly committed to the cause or just jumping on the latest bandwagon.

Oakley's 9/11 commemorative range sunglasses and Pepsi's 'Live for Now' campaign linked to Black Lives Matter attracted fierce criticism for their lack of authentic commitment and apparent brand washing with popular causes.[3] There is also a significant cost involved by the corporate to redesign packaging (which can negatively affect their product sales) or create dedicated products. That means more of the partnership budget is spent internally by the corporate instead of going to your non-profit.

It has also become a way for corporates to raise brand awareness by spending their consumers' cash. It may give the consumer an opportunity to benefit a favourite cause, but unless it's backed up by a significant commitment from the corporate, then the non-profit can attract some unwelcome criticism. The unrelenting scrutiny of corporate brands on social media means that a negative campaign can quickly take hold. This poses some significant risks for non-profits in choosing the right corporate partner and mitigating the potential downsides of association if things change.

Cause-related marketing can deliver some great results for a non-profit, but the team needs a degree of commercial acumen to manage them effectively. If philanthropy and sponsorships are like one-night stands, then cause-related marketing is more like a 'friends with benefits' relationship. Both sides are getting something out of the exchange, but it's unlikely to be sustainable over the longer term.

Social purpose driven partnerships

Social purpose explodes the old paradigm of a business existing simply to make a profit. Social purpose sees business as an engine for good, creating societal benefit in the way that business is done. Customers, consumers and the community have higher expectations of the role of business and it's keeping corporate CEOs awake at night. Corporates can't do this by themselves; they need non-profits to be part of the solution.

Social purpose partnerships go far beyond traditional philanthropy, sponsorships or cause-related marketing. Whilst any of them could be part of the implementation mix, it's rarely the whole story. If corporates are to demonstrate their authentic and sustainable commitment to a better world, they'll need to bring all their resources, skills, assets and strengths to the table. This presents a much bigger opportunity for non-profits but requires a shift in thinking from an exchange of value to a willingness to collaborate and co-create solutions. For corporates and non-profits in a well-constructed, strategically aligned partnership, this could be the marriage that leads to the golden wedding anniversary.

The impact of COVID-19 and the cost-of-living crisis

At a time when wages are stagnant, giving is constrained and the economic environment is uncertain, non-profits are being asked to do more with less. The need for community services has grown exponentially. In 2021-2022, Foodbank provided one million meals per month to Australians experiencing food insecurity, with 60% finding it more challenging than ever to make ends meet.[4] The Centre for Social Impact's 2021 Pulse Report showed that 77% of non-profit organisations stated that the COVID pandemic had put a strain on their finances, whilst 52% were worried about being unable to provide their services.[5]

Non-profits are exploring corporate partnerships, some for the first time, to provide the growth and income they need to meet soaring demand for their services. That means pressure on fundraising and partnership teams to deliver urgent results. Non-profit boards and CEOs are focusing on corporate partnerships as the antidote to unpredictable government funding or community giving. The Reset 2020 research showed that around 30% of charities were looking for new strategies to engage partners and 44% were seeking help in retaining existing partners and sponsors.[6]

But developing corporate partnerships has changed radically over the years, and non-profit leaders' understanding hasn't kept pace. They are often stuck in the old paradigm of case-for-support philanthropy, sponsorships or cause-related marketing. Their lack of education and personal experience with corporate partnerships often leads to less sophisticated and less effective approaches to the challenge.

These different terminologies often cause confusion in corporate partnerships. Later in this book,

> Non-profit boards and CEOs are focusing on corporate partnerships as the antidote to unpredictable government funding or community giving.

we'll outline a model for how to think about bringing together the different activities to create a unified partnership. It will de-mystify what a partnership could look like and how you can be successful.

The spectrum of corporate approaches to partnerships

If you feel like you're struggling to understand how partnerships have changed, you're not the only one. Corporates, too, are at different stages of evolution in responding to the pressures of societal expectations and business priorities. Not everyone is ready yet for thoughtful, strategic partnerships, but those who have taken the leap are seeing standout results for their competitive positioning, profitability and business goals.

The spectrum of responses looks like this.

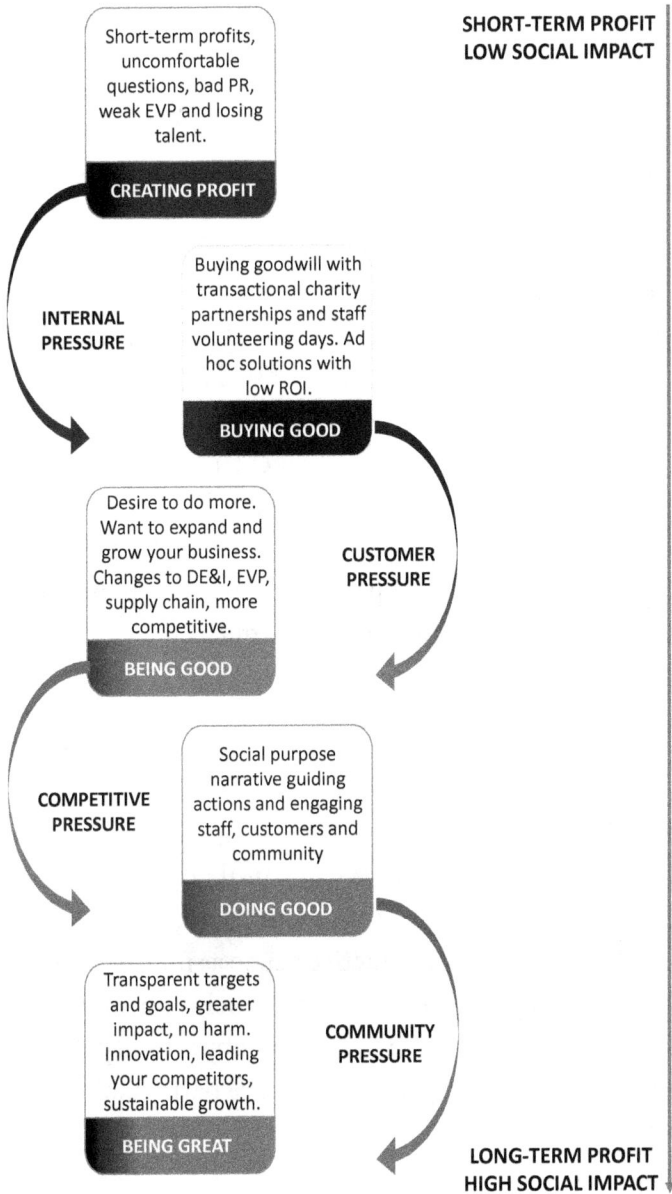

Short-term profits, uncomfortable questions, bad PR, weak EVP and losing talent.

CREATING PROFIT

SHORT-TERM PROFIT
LOW SOCIAL IMPACT

INTERNAL PRESSURE

Buying goodwill with transactional charity partnerships and staff volunteering days. Ad hoc solutions with low ROI.

BUYING GOOD

Desire to do more. Want to expand and grow your business. Changes to DE&I, EVP, supply chain, more competitive.

BEING GOOD

CUSTOMER PRESSURE

COMPETITIVE PRESSURE

Social purpose narrative guiding actions and engaging staff, customers and community

DOING GOOD

Transparent targets and goals, greater impact, no harm. Innovation, leading your competitors, sustainable growth.

BEING GREAT

COMMUNITY PRESSURE

LONG-TERM PROFIT
HIGH SOCIAL IMPACT

Figure 2: The spectrum of corporate responses

Some businesses are narrowly focused on creating profit, not social impact. However, these businesses are dealing with some uncomfortable questions about their lack of commitment to the community. This leads to poor brand image, a weak employee value proposition and costly churn in valuable employees and customers.

In response to this internal pressure, businesses typically respond by 'buying good'. This manifests in transactional non-profit partnerships, such as low-level corporate donations, one-off fundraising campaigns and tactical staff volunteering. Non-profits may benefit from some program funding or staff donations, but the relationship may not progress to more valuable relationships. Harvesting the additional income and support can be useful, but non-profits need to be careful not to expend too much energy or focus on these ad hoc partnerships.

Corporates face pressure from customers and investors to articulate their responses to societal issues. External stakeholders demand evidence of a corporate's social responsibility beyond a few tactical donations or PR campaigns. That leads to corporates making positive changes to their internal business practices, such as improved working conditions, enhanced diversity and inclusion or improved environmental impact. This is an opportunity for non-profits to offer their expertise and move partnerships beyond philanthropic donations.

Competitive pressure encourages corporates to lift their game in social responsibility. Just as non-profits can experience partnership envy, corporates want to share in the enormous benefits experienced by businesses developing strong social purpose programs. This leads them to seek more strategic partnerships with non-profits. They want your help to make a meaningful social impact that will be recognised as authentic and genuine by their staff, customers and suppliers. Not every business is accountable to external investors, but even medium-sized private businesses need a strong social responsibility narrative to be competitive.

The most ambitious and forward-thinking corporates are responding to community expectations by changing how they do business. This creates a unique competitive advantage for them and has the potential for transformational change in society. This is where great partnerships are created and sustained and why your non-profit needs to be ready for the opportunity.

> You don't want to be selling a Ferrari to someone who only wants a scooter.

Not every corporate wants to be transformational, but there is value for non-profits to work with them at every stage of their evolution. Your job is to understand their stage of development and be prepared to adapt to their needs and desired outcomes. Adapt your time, energy and focus to the type of opportunity on offer. You don't want to be selling a Ferrari to someone who only wants a scooter.

Typical responses from non-profits

Just as businesses have approached corporate partnerships differently, there is also a range of ways in which non-profits have tackled corporate partnerships.

Hire and hope

Non-profits that are enthusiastic about the untapped opportunity from corporate partnerships often respond by hiring a partnership manager and giving them a big KPI (key performance indicator). A senior leader once told us to 'Just get me $1 million and a helicopter'. Usually, the KPI has an unrealistic timeframe, i.e. less than 12 months, and then it's all about cash income. It's based on the need for the non-profit to fill an urgent gap in funding, not a realistic, thoughtful assessment of organisational needs or the likely opportunity.

It's a very unpleasant and stressful situation for the new partnership manager. They report regularly to a leadership that knows very little about how corporate partnerships work but is constantly pressing for results. The partnership manager's colleagues see them working long hours but don't understand how to have a role in their success. It's impossible for the partnership manager to succeed without the right organisational support. It becomes a very lonely role and the potential for burnout is high. The partnership manager resigns and the organisation hires another staff member. The cycle starts again.

Hiring great people is a good start, but the organisation must be ready for partnerships. It also needs to put in place appropriate training, development and organisational support for partnerships, rather than leave them to one lone ranger working by themselves.

Spray and pray

Another typical response from non-profits is the 'spray and pray' approach. That assumes high-value corporate partnerships are a numbers game, like selling consumer goods. This entails the corporate partnership manager sending out unsolicited proposals or making a high volume of calls to businesses of all kinds, in the hope that some will say yes. It's often a companion to the 'hire and hope' method but is typically augmented by activity-based KPIs.

Linda once met a newly appointed partnership manager in a health charity who had a KPI of making 50 new cold calls per week. Not follow-up calls or account management calls, but cold calls. He had worked through most of the ASX-listed organisations by the time she met him, and he was getting desperate enough to start on the local high street businesses nearby.

Corporate partnerships are not about numbers; they're about relationships. If a non-profit won't take time to understand the corporate's needs, priorities and perspectives, then why should the corporate respond? One Corporate Social Responsibility (CSR) manager at a large corporate received over 30 unsolicited proposals every month, and 29 of them went straight into the bin. The non-profits hadn't bothered to check if the proposal was relevant to her organisation and hadn't made contact before sending the proposal. It was the partnership equivalent of turning up to a blind date in a wedding dress. No wonder they failed at the first hurdle.

Accidental brilliance

If you hire someone and just give them a big KPI, the chances are that smart people will try their best to be successful. They may get lucky with some unsolicited approaches from corporates, or they may get some early wins with smaller partnerships. However, accidental brilliance isn't a sustainable strategy long term.

What typically happens is that the partnership portfolio gets filled with energy suckers: lots of small relationships that suck up the non-profit's time, attention, and resources for not much ROI. The time required to service these high-maintenance relationships prevents the organisation from thinking strategically or prospecting for more valuable partnerships.

It's hard to get your head above water when you're busy keeping so many small boats afloat at the same time. The level of frustration rises, both for the partnership manager and the non-profit leadership who want to see growth. Burnout inevitably leads to high staff turnover, which in turn compromises the continuity of relationship management. It's a cycle of frustration that needs a fresh approach.

Investing in experience

Experienced partnership managers are worth the investment if you're committed to supporting their growth and giving them the right environment to succeed. A tenacious and resilient partnership manager will be quick to learn and can put the underlying processes and systems in place. Building a thriving partnerships program takes time because the decision-making processes are dictated by corporate budgeting cycles. It takes 12-18 months to win new partners, so the non-profit needs to set appropriate timeframes and expectations for success.

Strategic and thoughtful

The best organisations are taking a more thoughtful and strategic approach to partnerships. That means investing in the right staff and providing appropriate support and development opportunities. Non-profits that succeed in corporate partnerships have moved away from the traditional models of philanthropy, sponsorship and cause-related marketing to explore collaborative partnerships that deliver business value and social impact. Modern partnerships are less about an exchange of value and more about creating new value together.

When the Sydney Biennale partnered with property developers Mirvac for a five-year partnership, it wasn't about ticket sales and sponsorship.[7] The core of the partnership was a commitment to enriching urban life and making art and culture accessible to everyone. It was strategic, thoughtful and much more valuable to the non-profit, the corporate and the community in the longer term.

If you want to be successful in corporate partnerships, create transformational change and tap into this growing revenue stream, take a long-term strategic approach.

Corporates need you to be the solution

Businesses face unprecedented scrutiny from consumers, employees, investors and governments in addition to the day-to-day challenges of maintaining profitable operations in uncertain economic times. Levels of trust in governments and media are plummeting and businesses are being asked to step in to fill the gaps left by government inaction.

Edelman Trust Barometer's global research of 35,000 people across 25 countries shows that business CEOs are now expected to take the lead on societal change. Some 86% of employees think it's important that their CEO speaks out and takes action on big societal issues, including inequality, training for future jobs, diversity and the environment. In addition, 78% think CEOs should take the lead on change rather than wait for the government to drive it, and 62% believe CEOs should publicly hold the government accountable for their decisions.[8]

Business leaders carry high expectations from the community to take urgent and meaningful action. If they don't, 62%

of employees and 67% of consumers believe they have the power to force corporates to change. The pressure is intense.

If economic instability and business operations weren't challenging enough, problems such as discrimination, climate change, inequality and job security are now on the Must Do list for businesses. They can't do this by themselves. Although the Edelman research shows that corporates are now viewed as the most competent institutions worldwide, non-profits are still considered the most ethical and trustworthy.

A partnership with your non-profit could help to achieve meaningful social impact and meet the expectations of employees, investors, stakeholders and consumers. Corporates need your non-profit more than ever before. If corporates are to meet those lofty expectations and remain competitive, they will need the expertise, audiences, assets, networks, and credibility of non-profits to help them do it. Make sure your non-profit is ready to seize the opportunity.

Could corporates achieve their goals without your partnership? They don't lack the resources and the community sees them as more competent than governments in driving social change. Non-profits don't have a monopoly on ethics. Corporates are setting up their own foundations and collaborating with social enterprises to create new ways of addressing social issues. It's unlikely that corporates will become competitors with your non-profit, but they want partners who work with them strategically to solve the big social issues.

CASE STUDY
Beyond Blue and Australia Post

Beyond Blue is one of Australia's largest and well-known mental health charities. Its core mission is to help all Australians experience their best mental health through education, awareness, advocacy and support services. There was already a growing crisis in mental health before COVID-19, with over three million Australians experiencing anxiety or depression.[9] The pandemic, combined with drought, bushfires and economic instability, meant that Beyond Blue experienced a 58% increase in demand for their services in 2020 and over one million people visited their online support forums. There was an urgent need to meet the soaring demand.

Beyond Blue turned to corporate partners for help. They didn't seek traditional philanthropy or sponsorship, but instead sought a partner to help them expand their reach across Australia. Australia Post was the perfect fit. Australia Post is at the heart of communities in every corner of Australia, connecting people through their 4,000 Post Offices, daily deliveries and communications. The organisation's ethos and social purpose were all about their commitment to community and being there for Australians in need.

The partnership did include financial support but went much further. Every Australia Post delivery van now has a Beyond Blue logo, prompting Australians to seek help. Australia Post has delivered more than six million leaflets about mental health, providing education, awareness and information, and helping to de-stigmatise anxiety and depression. Australia Post even created a special postage stamp, 'When we connect, we feel better', and four million pre-paid postcards as part of the partnership.[10]

The partnership achieved what neither organisation could do by themselves. It leveraged the skills, strengths, expertise and assets of both organisations to encourage Australians to seek help with mental health. If Beyond Blue had taken a more traditional approach, it would have simply asked Australia Post for a donation to help with marketing and education campaigns. Taking a more strategic approach to both the choice of partner and the approach to the partnership meant they could create a much better solution together.

Conclusion

Edelman's research shows that 46% of respondents expect that private-public partnerships are key to addressing societal challenges. Partnerships will bring innovations, progress, improvements in the world and positive impacts on the way that we interact with each other. Big, thorny societal issues can't be solved by one organisation or even one sector. The case for working in partnership has never been more urgent and the opportunity to transform not just business but society is greater than ever before. Partnerships can take time and effort, but the rewards are exponentially better than simple fundraising.

> 'In times of change, learners will inherit the earth while the learned will find themselves beautifully equipped to deal with a world that no longer exists'.

It's time for non-profits to step into the spotlight and embrace the partnerships revolution. As the American philosopher Eric Hoffer wrote, 'In times of change, learners will inherit the earth while the learned will find themselves beautifully equipped to deal with a world that no longer exists'.

The Opportunity
for Non-profits

The size of the opportunity is growing

Research from JBWere in The Corporate Support Report outlines the evolution of corporate giving and clearly shows that the size of the prize for non-profits is growing. Data from the USA shows rapid growth in corporate giving over the last 50 years, correlating strongly to company pre-tax profits. The proportion of corporate giving as community investment has averaged 0.9% of pre-tax profit.[1]

In Australia, JBWere's research on the top 50 corporates has shown similarly impressive growth. During the worst of the COVID pandemic, when Australia's economy was also struggling with devastating bushfires, corporate profits declined by 30%, yet corporate giving rose by 23%. The growth continued into 2021. It is estimated that corporate community investment in Australia is now worth around $5 billion per annum.

It's an impressive total, but why are so many non-profits failing to capitalise on this gold mine of cash and other support? JBWere asserts that 'the link between business and the for-purpose sector is... perhaps the least understood'. Perhaps the legacy of the fundraising mindset has held back non-profits from pursuing the most significant opportunities.

> 'The link between business and the for-purpose sector is... perhaps the least understood.'

The non-profits that have invested in corporate partnerships yielded some of the greatest returns during tough times. Joint research by five agencies looking at the impact of COVID-19 on fundraising across different activities saw corporate partnerships as a stand-out performer.[2] During the first four months of the pandemic, income received by non-profits from corporates increased by 51%, with a median increase of 33%. Some non-profits in the survey reported a doubling in their income from corporate partners as long-term partners stepped up to offer significant support.

The game has changed for corporates

The corporate appetite for partnerships has grown. The investor focus on environment, social and governance (ESG) measures has meant that corporates are shifting to community partnerships as a way to meet their goals. The ESG metrics are embedded in the individual KPIs of business leaders and are used to compare the performance of companies against their competitors.

Many corporates rely on their non-profit partners to provide the evidence of impact and outcomes needed to meet the ESG standards. It means a shift towards real social impact and the need for investment beyond traditional corporate philanthropy. The ESG drivers are relevant for the larger, publicly listed corporates and their unlisted, medium-sized competitors. The smaller players may not have investors, but they do need a strong narrative to match the competition.

Beyond ESG, the game has changed for corporates seeking government contracts. Federal and state governments in Australia and across the world are making social impact a key requirement of their business procurement.[3] Various states have legislated requirements that range from gender equity, diversity and inclusion or environmental impacts for corporates tendering for contracts. Partnerships with non-profits are important for corporates to help navigate these requirements and make sure they have a compelling narrative, meaningful impact and measurable outcomes. Given the size of government contracts, there is a huge opportunity for non-profits to demonstrate the commercial value of a corporate-community partnership and position themselves for much greater commitments from corporates.

In the latest research from Edelman, corporate entities are still viewed as the most competent, but corporates are rapidly closing the gap on non-profits in perceptions of ethics. Non-profits must seek partnerships with the corporate sector before corporates start to explore the options of doing it by themselves.[4]

Taking the F-word out of partnerships

The F-word in partnerships is fundraising. Corporate partnerships are typically the awkward teenagers in the non-profit family; they look familiar, but it's an uneasy fit. That's why partnerships are usually corralled into fundraising. However, treating corporate partnerships as fundraising can lead to misguided approaches and a lot of wasted time and effort. Here's why.

> The F-word in partnerships is fundraising.

Low impact for lots of effort

If your non-profit leads with a fundraising approach (similar to a case for support with major donors), you usually present a program or service for funding. But then you're stuck. You are limited to the amount you can spend on that project.

In order to meet your financial KPIs, you're forced to find more corporate 'donors' to hit those targets. It means you end up with a portfolio of small-scale, low-value partnerships that burn your time and effort. You're also unlikely to get the impact you seek for your cause. The other risk is that corporate philanthropy is a small bucket of money that's shrinking fast. In tough economic environments, philanthropy is vulnerable to budget cuts as it's regarded as discretionary spend. Your program or service could be on shaky ground if it relies solely on corporate philanthropy.

It's all about me, not we

Partnerships should be an invitation to collaborate and make a meaningful impact on a social issue together. Fundraising is just a bilateral transaction, an exchange of money and goods. A corporate partner gives you some of its plentiful resources and your non-profit tries to create some good with it.

We worked with a charity that convinced a large energy company to support 100 sponsorships for girls' education in Uganda. It was lucrative annual income that boosted the partnership team's KPIs. However, the energy company had no alignment with the work in Uganda and no participation other than the annual payment. When management changed, they couldn't find a single reason to keep supporting these sponsorships. Instead, they switched to supporting valuable work for disadvantaged families in regional Victoria, where they operated. The new partnership enabled them to offer volunteers, skills and support to make a real impact on local families.

If you're only focused on fundraising and meeting financial KPIs, then it's too easy to forget that it's called partnerships. Partners work together to make a lasting impact in the ecosystem they both inhabit. Connections, reciprocity and mutual support will help everyone in the ecosystem thrive and grow.

Switch the conversation from fundraising to partnerships. Build relationships that invite your partner into a collaboration. If you obsess over the F-word that is fundraising, you'll get stuck in a cycle of frustration that will burn time, resources and staff effort. Time to bury that F-word for good.

Getting the full value of partnerships

Treating partnerships as purely financial transactions is like turning up at a five-star restaurant and choosing chips and gravy. You're missing out on the wealth of other value and impact that comes with a deeper, strategic relationship with a corporate. Of course, your non-profit needs money and we all love to see a big cheque. But in the urgent search for fundraising income, you can miss out on bigger buckets of value that could create more impact for your charity.

> Many types of value can be gained from a corporate partnership.

Lead with the value you offer and the impact you can both create and the money will come, but if you lead with your fundraising gap, you may never unlock the untapped value that lies below.

Many types of value can be gained from a corporate partnership beyond cash.

Networks and audiences

A corporate partner will have broader reach, more marketing and different channels to help a non-profit access new and valuable audiences.

When mental health charity R U OK? partnered with Sensis and Yellow Pages, it put the charity on the front page of five million directories across Australia and the Sensis online platform.[5] As an organisation dedicated to raising awareness of and combating the stigma of poor mental health, the impact on the charity was so much greater than simply asking for money.

There was certainly significant cash in the partnership to fund some specific programs, but R U OK? and Yellow have followed with dedicated resources for small business owners and tradies – a notoriously difficult demographic to reach with mental health messages. If R U OK? had simply asked for money, they would have funded some small-scale advertising themselves. Now, through the partnership, they're reaching millions of people each day.

Skills and expertise

Lifeline Australia works in suicide prevention and helps over a million Australians seeking crisis support every year. During the pandemic, the need for services soared and they received a call every 15 seconds. At the same time, Lifeline's system wasn't equipped to allow their workforce of trained volunteers to work remotely. One in ten calls went unanswered when people were facing their most desperate times. Lifeline partnered with Cisco, a large technology company, which used its core skills and expertise to deploy remote working capabilities for over 10,000 crisis support workers.[6] They also created a text functionality to make Lifeline's services more accessible. Lifeline leveraged what Cisco does well – using technology to create connections and, through the partnership, helped save lives.

Media, PR and marketing

Australian Childhood Foundation (ACF) supports children and families to rebuild their lives after abuse, neglect and family violence. Their partnership with major retailer Target Australia came with a minimum guarantee of $250,000 in cash but yielded a heap of other value.[7] ACF could leverage Target's media, marketing and communications channels to reach an audience of staff, customers and followers. Prominence in Target's store network, social media, newsletters, website, advertising and communications allowed ACF's resources to reach deeper into the community and created increased awareness for the organisation's work. The partnership enabled ACF to tap into a much larger marketing and promotional budget than they could have afforded alone.

Non-cash value and volunteers

Ronald McDonald House Charities (RMHC) provide essential care to seriously ill children and their families when they have to travel far from home to access medical care. RMHC couldn't run their houses without their corporate partners. Partners provide in-kind support for everything required in the house, from beds, mattresses and toilet paper to teabags and toys. In addition to staff and customer fundraising, the corporate partners are also a reliable pipeline of volunteers to help run the houses. Corporate teams cook meals, clean houses and offer mentoring support to families. The value of RMHC's corporate partners goes far beyond cash income and helps to relieve a significant amount of the organisation's operational costs.

Advocacy

Activist groups worked for years to advance marriage equality in Australia. When a plebiscite was announced in 2017, the Australian Marriage Equality (AME) group inspired corporates to become advocates for the campaign. Corporates used their PR, marketing and channels to amplify the case for a Yes vote and inspire the community to back the campaign. Business leaders and CEOs of companies from Qantas to Coca-Cola became vocal advocates for the cause and offered substantial in-kind assistance, including travel, advertising, office space and legal advice to AME.[8] Getting more than 850 corporates to work with AME helped to amplify and augment community voices and ensured an overwhelming Yes.

Research and innovation

Harnessing research and innovation requires real trust from both partners because they are sharing their valuable intellectual property for the greater good. Undertaking joint research about something that is impacting your beneficiaries can also create benefits for a corporate partner.

Reckitt Benckiser worked with Save the Children to examine the cause of diarrhoea in emerging economies, as diarrhoea was the biggest killer of young children.[9] They focused on India and the barriers to hand washing. The principal issues were cost and behaviour change, so Reckitt Benckiser created beautiful perfumed soaps in small and affordable packages and worked with Save the Children experts to encourage people to wash their hands regularly. Reckitt Benckiser created a new product and a new market for their goods and improved the health of thousands of children. These kinds of innovations have created real and lasting change in people's lives. Neither organisation would have focused on it without the other partner and they created a far bigger impact than simply raising funds for the non-profit.

Partnerships as an ecosystem

Getting the full value requires a shift in polarised thinking from 'them and us' to just 'us'. Only then can true relationships, partnerships and trust be built for the benefit of non-profits, corporates and the community.

Linda spent her childhood exploring the ancient forests around London, where complex networks and partnerships exist in old growth forests that scientists call the 'wood-wide web'.[10] It's a perfect example of how the best corporate-community partnerships thrive and why some never make it past infancy. There are four things we can learn from the wood-wide web.

1. It's all one ecosystem

In an old growth forest, the trees, plants and fungi form underground partnerships that are intricately connected. Just as in human society, we all have an impact on our community and our needs are interdependent. Corporates and non-profits may speak a slightly different language, but are equally part of the same ecosystem. Creating partnerships that improve the ecosystem we all inhabit will be more valuable and more impactful long term than prioritising the needs of one type of organisation over the other.

2. Reciprocity ensures that everyone thrives

Researchers have found that every tree in the forest is linked. They share carbon, water, nutrients and other resources with each other, with the oldest and biggest trees frequently sending more to help the youngest and smallest. The younger reciprocate when older trees are struggling. In partnerships, it's too easy to think of corporates as the giant redwoods and keep tapping them for resources to support your non-profit. Non-profits must consider what they can offer in return and how that will not just meet short-term needs in tough economic times, but nurture and strengthen the connections for the future. The strongest partnerships display the generosity, reciprocity and constant negotiation that helps the forest to thrive.

3. The less connected ones struggle to survive

Seedlings planted in isolation from the forest's lifelines of support are less likely to survive than their networked counterparts. Think of the big challenges your non-profit is trying to address, such as homelessness, poverty, inequality, climate change and more. You may make some early progress by yourself, but your sapling won't become an old growth giant if you're not connected. Seek out the corporate partners that are best connected to your values, mission and ambitions and you'll grow faster and further than you can alone. Find the connections that nourish both organisations and you'll transform the forest at the same time.

4. Competition doesn't mean greater progress

Taking a Darwinian view, you'd think that each tree competes for resources to ensure its own survival. But the forest isn't a pitched battle; it's a place for sophisticated negotiation, communication and collaboration. Far from being a competition for dominance or kudos; corporate-community partnerships are a collaborative effort to find new ways of creating social progress. The best partnerships are a win-win-win for corporates, non-profits and the community.

The next time you find yourself deep in the tranquillity of a forest, think of the millions of sophisticated exchanges, negotiations and communications being conducted under your feet. If you'd like human society to live as richly as an old growth forest then make sure your partnerships are just as connected, reciprocal and mutually invested. To do that, take a leap in thinking away from the old paradigms of corporate partnerships and towards more integrated and rewarding relationships.

> Corporate-community partnerships are a collaborative effort

Harnessing the opportunity

Corporate partnerships have the potential to be transformational for non-profits and their partners. There is untapped value in collaboration to achieve better social outcomes, better organisational performance and sustainable impact on society. As Figure 3 illustrates, non-profits need to step beyond a fundraising mindset and embrace the many benefits that strategically aligned partnerships can offer.

Transactional relationship with businesses. In exchange for program funding, they receive set benefits.

PROGRAM SUPPORT

TRANSACTIONAL PARTNERSHIPS LOW SOCIAL IMPACT

TIED FUNDING

Additional value and depth of relationship is created through WPG, engagement and employee fundraising.

EMPLOYEE ENGAGEMENT

Be a solution to business ambitions and challenges, with consumer-facing activations and content.

PARTNERSHIP SOLUTIONS

ADDITIONAL VALUE

UNTIED FUNDING

Peer-to-peer relationships, with a deep trust and sharing of assets and IP to achieve measurable outcomes.

STRATEGIC

A coalition relationship model with new solutions designed and implemented together.

STELLAR

COMPOUND RETURNS

TRANSFORMATIONAL PARTNERSHIPS HIGH SOCIAL IMPACT

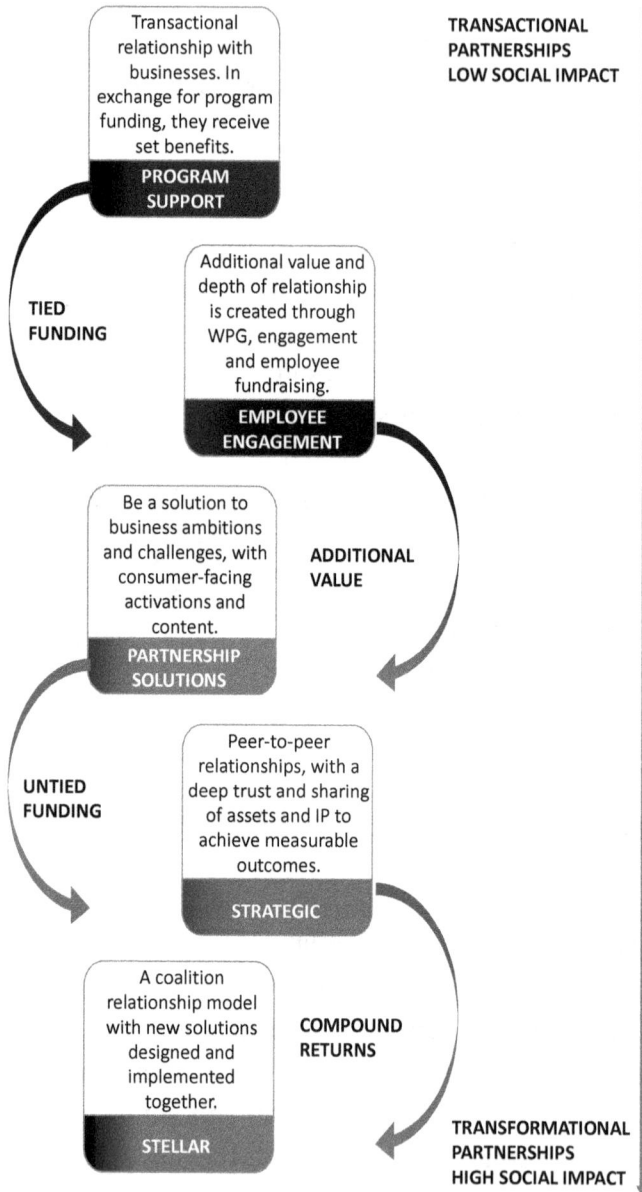

Figure 3: From transaction to transformation

When non-profits get stuck in the program funding and philanthropy paradigm, the relationship with a corporate partner is simply a transaction. The support is restricted to one or two programs and the non-profit might be lucky enough to add 10% for operational costs. Once the program is finished, so is the relationship, and it's unlikely that there will be long-term value for either party. This approach is often found in organisations that are comfortable with grants from philanthropic foundations and have applied the same approach to their corporate partnerships. It's a recipe for high churn in their partnerships as the relationship has little depth.

In order to extend the relationship, non-profits typically offer their partners employee engagement and volunteering opportunities. That enables them to unlock additional income through staff fundraising and the volunteering may assist with some basic operations. In many cases, however, the non-profit fails to properly assign the cost of managing volunteers, creating activities and taking time from new prospect development. The partnership is an exchange of value, where both parties get something out of the relationship, but it hasn't created a significant impact on society.

A more collaborative partnership can often develop in brand and marketing campaigns, where a corporate derives more commercial benefit from sales and customer engagement. Collaboration allows the non-profit to access greater income, brand awareness and audiences from the partnership. It deepens the relationship and starts to create more social impact.

The optimal state for a corporate partnership is a strategically aligned relationship that allows the co-creation of both the partnership pillars and the desired outcomes. Rather than a transaction or exchange of value, the corporate partner is invited to create the future with the non-profit. This can be challenging for many non-profits who are used to being the experts in their field. It's nice to be the heroes of the story, doing their world-changing work if only a corporate partner can provide the funds. But it's not great for a long-term partnership and doesn't empower the corporate partner to contribute all of the assets, strengths, skills and services they can offer. It requires a shift in thinking from 'us and them' to simply 'us'.

> More than two-thirds of the richest 100 entities in the world are corporates.

The shift in thinking to an 'us' mindset requires non-profits to put themselves in the shoes of their corporate partner and gain a deep understanding of their competitive landscape and internal dynamics. Sometimes this deters many non-profits from pursuing corporate partnership opportunities. It's unfamiliar or unknown territory and those shoes can feel extremely uncomfortable.

A new, strategic approach to partnerships will unleash the full potential of the corporate sector to contribute to meaningful social change. Many global corporates are larger and more powerful than governments. More than two-thirds of the richest 100 entities in the world are corporates, not governments.[11] Government support can also be mercurial and unpredictable. If non-profits want to solve some of society's thorniest problems, there is no time to lose. It's time to reimagine partnerships.

CASE STUDY
Fujitsu and Camp Quality

Fujitsu is a global information and communications technology company. For five years, it partnered with Camp Quality, an Australian charity working with kids affected by cancer and their families. Over the years, Fujitsu developed a close relationship with Camp Quality, hosting various events and raising over $500,000 to help children and their families with their journey through cancer.

When COVID-19 struck, Camp Quality could not run their normal face-to-face operations with children but still needed to provide quality support programs. Fujitsu found a way to use technology to solve the problem. By leveraging their expertise in a unique form of design thinking, Fujitsu's Digital Transformation Centre worked closely with Camp Quality to find innovative solutions. The result was an on-demand digital service and app to support children and families in their cancer journey.[12] The Kids Guide to Cancer app is a free educational program that answers the key questions that kids have about cancer, delivered in a way that's accessible and age-appropriate.

Camp Quality has built on a solid relationship over time to fully leverage the core skills, expertise, innovation and assets of Fujitsu. The impact on vulnerable children and families has been so much greater than fundraising alone.

Conclusion

For too long, corporate partnerships have been the wallflowers on the dance floor whilst the cool kids danced with fundraising. The growing needs of society, their enhanced expectations of the corporate sector and a turbulent post-COVID economy mean we must bring all resources to bear on the world's thorniest problems. It's time for corporate partnerships to step out of the shadows and into the spotlight and for non-profits to harness the untapped opportunities waiting.

3

FIND New Partners

One of our children's favourite bedtime books was *Are You My Mother?*. A baby bird hatches from his nest while his mother is away, and he sets out to find her. He has no idea what she looks like, so he asks everyone he meets, 'Are you my mother?'. On the journey, he meets some unlikely candidates, including a cow, a dog and even a plane, before a final happy reunion with his mum.

When non-profits start to explore corporate partnerships, they can take a similarly hit-and-miss approach. They start with a big, ambitious income target and work through the largest listed companies. Many months and years of effort are wasted talking to organisations that aren't interested or the right fit. Partnerships are not a numbers game, like consumer goods sales or acquiring individual donors. They are strategic relationships that must be carefully chosen, well-aligned and built on common objectives. If you want valuable partnerships that sustain and grow, take a strategic approach. Accidental brilliance is not a strategy, nor is starting with the top 200 listed companies and working through from A-Z.

The potential for corporate-community partnerships is being frustrated by the poor choices non-profits make about partners. Good luck or accidental brilliance may result in some early small wins, but organisations quickly become locked in a cycle of frustration (Figure 4) that burns relationships, goodwill and staff. The full potential of partnerships is never realised, and leadership is reluctant to invest further.

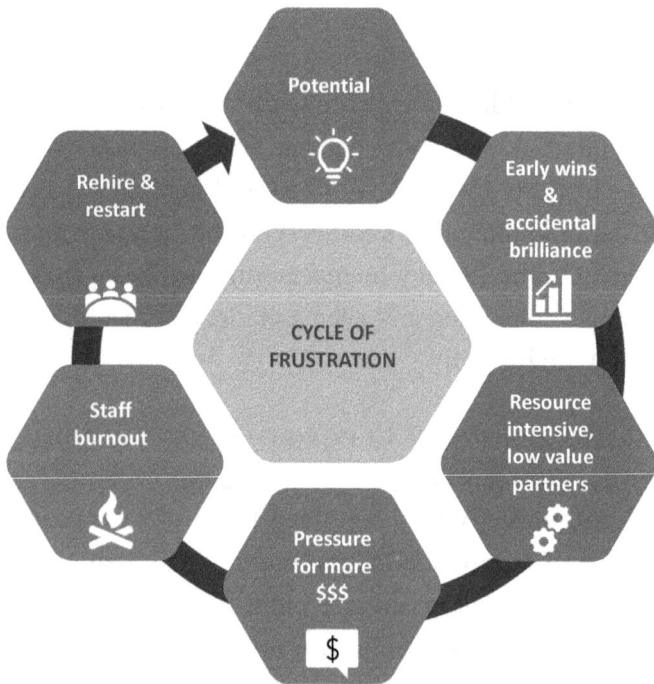

Figure 4: Cycle of frustration

Build the strategic foundations first. It's the best way to achieve significant, long-lasting partnerships and avoid churning good staff. These foundations ensure that the choice of future corporate partners is aligned with your own strategy, needs and ambitions. You're talking to the wrong partners if they don't deliver on your core mission and help you get where you want. You may get some short-term income uplift, but ultimately, they'll destroy value. Building strategic foundations ensures the biggest return for your scarce resources, time and effort.

> Build the strategic foundations first.

There are four key steps to FINDing the right corporate partner: Focus, Identify, Navigate and Decide.

Decide	4	A strategically aligned prospect shortlist
Navigate	3	No go areas and a tailored risk framework
Identify	2	Your unique offering and the value you bring
Focus	1	Where you are going and what you need from a partner

Figure 5: Key steps to FINDing the right corporate partner

FOCUS

Corporates expect that your organisation needs money. But your funding gap is not a reason for them to partner with you. They are more interested in the impact you want to achieve for society and how they can help.

Corporates have a range of strengths, assets and skills to bring to a partnership. Your non-profit needs to think broadly about how to fully leverage what a corporate has to offer and how that will transform your mission. Regarding corporate partnerships simply as free cash is like going to a breakfast buffet and just ordering toast. You'll be missing out on the other delicious helpings of value they have to offer. By connecting with a corporate on areas besides money, you'll create a partnership with multiple points of relationship. Not only will you achieve a bigger impact, but you'll entrench the relationship over the longer term. Then the money will follow and it's likely to be a bigger commitment than just a one-off donation.

Unpack the following areas to discover the full range of your needs and be able to describe the impact that a partnership could achieve.

Strengths

What do you do well and what is your organisation known for? It might be your specialist expertise, loyal tribe of followers or the unique space you inhabit. Perhaps you've won awards or important recognition. What do your staff, customers or the wider public perceive you as being the best at? This is a great opportunity to get the perspectives of people across your organisation. How is the world a better place because of the work you've done and the breakthroughs you've made? For every answer, consider WHY. Identify what makes you special, unique and credible as a future partner.

Opportunities

What's happening in the external environment that plays to your strengths or presents an opportunity? It could be a shift in public focus, government actions, latest research or demographic changes. For example, community pressure for action on gendered violence, the impact of COVID on mental health, the growing economic divide, a rise in homelessness or population shifts from metro to regional. Consider the opportunities, hot topics and gaps in the current environment and demonstrate how your organisation is part of the solution. Then, you'll have a strong proposition to a corporate for urgent action and a partnership with you.

Aspirations

Partnerships are a long-term investment of time, resources and commitment. Why should a corporate come on the journey with you if you can't articulate where you're going? As General Patton famously said, 'Without a strategy, you're just a tourist'. And tourists don't stay for long.

What are your goals for the next three, five and ten years? What would an ideal future look like? If you could wave a magic wand, what would you like to achieve?

Your goals might be long term and aspirational, but dreams and big ambitions can be very seductive to a corporate. They present a challenge and inspiration to a partner. Be clear on the future that a corporate partner will celebrate with you and shout it loudly to all their staff, customers and stakeholders. Great examples include Cancer Council Australia's goal to 'Eliminate cervical cancer by 2030' and Save the Children's aim to ensure that 'No child dies from preventable causes before their fifth birthday'.[1]

In contrast, some goals and ambitions clearly need work. Transforming people's lives for generations to come by creating infinite value' doesn't do justice to a respected international microfinance agency. Articulating your organisation's aspirations clearly and without jargon is the key to inspiring a potential corporate partner.

Needs

Corporates get that you need cash. But what else will transform your organisation and your impact? You understand your strengths, but what about your gaps and those squeaky wheel issues that are still on the wish list? It could be skills to manage multiple projects effectively, channels to help build awareness or volunteers to support program activities. A corporate has a wealth of assets to bring to a partnership, so think about which ones would help you fill your gaps or get you closer to achieving your big ambitions.

When the Garvan Institute for Medical Research secured a partnership with Vodafone, it wasn't to secure a donation.[2] They needed data to run their supercomputer faster and process research results. Their partnership with Vodafone created DreamLab, an app that captured unused data from customers' mobile phones while they were asleep. The processing power from idle smartphones has enabled Garvan to fast-track their cancer research and get them closer to their ambitious goals. If you are going to be the very best version of your organisation, what do you need?

Results

What does success look like? How do you know you're making progress? How can you describe or measure it? Corporate partners need you to paint a picture for them of the impact you've created together. They need to communicate success in a way that's accessible for their staff, customers, investors and audiences. Like the old saying, 'If a tree falls in the forest and no one is around to hear it, does it make a sound?', corporates need to celebrate and describe results publicly to demonstrate that the partnership was a worthy investment. In the growing ESG environment, it's also critical to their own success to have measurable outcomes and impact that translate to their ESG metrics.

By taking a thoughtful approach to partnerships, you'll be able to answer the four key questions that a corporate will ask you to determine whether you're worthy of consideration.

1. Where are you going?
2. What do you need?
3. Why me?
4. Why now?

If you cannot answer these key questions, you'll be presenting a cookie-cutter proposal that is not tailored to your corporate prospect. The prospect of getting past the first approach is low and you may not get a second chance. It will feel like those spam emails you receive daily; the only personalisation is the [insert name] function. By anchoring a partnership in your core strategy and future ambitions, you'll be able to tell a compelling story that answers those four key questions and makes your corporate partner an intrinsic part of your future success.

IDENTIFY

Once you've answered the four key questions, consider what you have to offer in return. There is a quid pro quo in corporate partnerships that goes beyond good will and cheap publicity. By cataloguing and evaluating your organisational assets, you'll be able to identify what's valuable to a corporate and which businesses might be interested in what you have to offer.

An asset catalogue is familiar to anyone who has worked in sponsorships. It is typically used with large sporting clubs, outlining assets such as TV rights, memberships, attendances and commercial value to future sponsors. But non-profits have a bunch of intangible assets that are not for sale or don't translate easily to commercial metrics. Instead, you're building a complete picture of what you bring to the table to solve a corporate's thorny problems, not just giving them a quick public relations sugar hit.

Gather this type of information from across your organisation.

What makes you special?	Your core expertise
	Your core programs
	Any awards or recognition
	Any key patrons, ambassadors or influencers that could enhance a partnership
	Your brand identity and values
Who do you talk to?	Your audiences, networks, followers and tribe. This includes social media engagement, website visits, donors, newsletters, advertising and media.
How do you connect?	Events, volunteer opportunities, campaigns or activations.
Where do you connect?	Your geographic footprint and reach, e.g. national, international, rural, regional or metro. That includes your programs and services, beneficiaries, offices, and outposts.

The key is gathering metrics, where possible, on every aspect of your asset catalogue. You can't tell a partner you've got a loyal and engaged audience if you can't describe or measure them. The devil is in the detail for assets, and this is where non-profits often lack the level of granularity needed. The more specific you can be, especially about your audiences, the easier it will be to identify and attract a partner who finds them valuable.

For example, Ovarian Cancer Australia has a strong and trusted profile with women aged 35-50. They hold a range of events during Ovarian Cancer Awareness Month and provide a unique set of expertise, resources, support and a helpline for anyone affected by ovarian cancer. It is a valuable audience for consumer brands targeting that cohort. The clarity on their audience and core assets means the organisation has successfully attracted corporate partners like Interflora, Hanes/Bonds and Fernwood Fitness, all of which target the same core female consumers.[3]

Understanding and cataloguing your assets will help you identify the hidden gems of value you can offer a corporate and who might be interested in them. It also enables you to filter out those that don't have an obvious alignment.

You will never share your full asset list with a partner. It is an internal catalogue of confidence that helps you unpack your offering and reshape it according to the priorities of your corporate partner. Different corporates will find different things valuable, just as some people will love gourmet food and fashion whilst others go crazy for walking boots and camping gear. By compiling your asset catalogue and keeping it regularly updated, you will be able to tailor and nuance your offer without reinventing the wheel each time.

Non-profits are often encouraged to get a valuation on their assets. This approach is problematic. There is no doubt that your assets are valuable, but that doesn't necessarily translate to a single price. When agencies offer a valuation, it's typically for the marketing assets only and it's a comparison to commercially offered alternatives. But this is only a fraction of the story and the true value to a corporate partner. In Chapter Four, we will explore in detail how to put a price on a partnership and a new way of thinking about value.

NAVIGATE

There are thousands of potential corporate partners. How do you know where to start? Which are the best fit for you? And how do you navigate this universe of possibilities? Typically, the best place to start is identifying the types of corporates that are *not* the right fit. Do this before you start conversations with corporates or you can find yourself in advanced conversations that can be awkward to terminate. Equally, you don't want to display your lack of preparation or internal processes before a prospective new partner.

One children's charity was approached by a bottled water company interested in a partnership. Whilst fresh water was a good fit for the charity's water and hygiene programs, there was concern over the environmental impact of plastic bottles. The charity had no risk framework for deciding on the partnership and, even worse, no one knew who had final decision rights. The issue bumped along from department to department without a decision until the prospective corporate partner got fed up and went elsewhere. A lose-lose situation for everyone.

A non-profit typically has few real assets beyond some modest financial reserves and its reputation. Putting in place a solid risk management framework will guide the choice of partners and prevent any potential reputational damage from the association with a company that does not match a non-profit's values. It will ensure consistency and efficiency of decision-making and enable the non-profit to manage expectations with prospective corporate partners.

First, consider the types of companies that are definitely on your no-go list. These are the ones that are a clear misfit for your values, your core mission and your beneficiaries. For example, a health charity might decide to exclude corporates whose primary business is tobacco, alcohol or junk food. Save the Children International had an embargo on companies promoting the use of infant formula in developing countries over breastfeeding, as the lack of clean water to mix with the formula was life-threatening for infants.[4] The list of no-go areas is specific to the non-profit and its mission and values. There can be no single list of inappropriate corporates, although the following sectors typically appear frequently:

- Armaments
- Tobacco

- Pornography
- Slave labour/illegal activities

The list of potentially controversial companies is always longer. These are corporates whose core business may present reputational risks or whose conduct has been less than exemplary. Again, the list is entirely personal to each non-profit. What evokes concern for one may be perfectly acceptable to another. The following are areas of concern that appear regularly on the potentially controversial list:

- Alcohol
- Junk food
- Gambling
- Environmental abuses
- Human rights abuses
- Dispossession or abuse of First Nations peoples' rights
- Exploitative credit practices
- Exploitative labour practices
- Unethical sales practices
- Mining and extraction
- Fossil fuels and coal seam gas/fracking
- Pending consumer class actions or legal sanctions
- Political parties and trade unions
- Crypto currencies

The list of potentially controversial corporate partners is intended to prompt deeper due diligence and investigation to ensure that there are ways to mitigate the risks of a partnership. Non-profits will deal with varying shades of grey with each partnership as no corporate is squeaky clean. It doesn't mean that you won't enter into a partnership, but the nature of that partnership may vary to minimise potential reputational damage for the non-profit. For example, you may choose not to enter into a public partnership with a tobacco company but accept workplace/payroll giving from their employees, so long as there is no company-matched donation and no public communication of any relationship. Equally, you may consider a company with a history of environmental missteps, but choose to work with them in an advocacy capacity to help reshape and improve their practices.

A robust policy document, agreed by leadership and board, will set the parameters for the organisation's risk appetite and give clear direction to partnership decisions in the future. There is no magic formula, but a non-profit should aim to have this in place before starting partnership prospecting.

DECIDE

In partnerships, unlike personal relationships, opposites don't attract. Non-profits must demonstrate why they are the natural fit for a corporate partner and why it will make sense for the corporate's staff, customers and stakeholders. Can you answer their key question, '*Why me?*' The community partnership manager at the large retailer Officeworks told of the unsolicited brochure she received from a well-known non-profit. It was slick, glossy and expensively produced. However, it ended up in the bin because there was no evidence that the non-profit had taken the time to understand the priorities of the business. It was a standard brochure that could have been sent to anyone.

Corporates make tough choices every day about where to invest their budget for the best impact. A non-profit must identify the synergies and rationale for a partnership to decide on the best-fit targets for future corporate opportunities. Once you've identified the fit, you'll have a much stronger and more compelling proposition for that corporate prospect.

The following are the primary areas of commonality to investigate:

Brand and personality

Each non-profit has a distinct brand identity. Some, like The Salvation Army, might be mature and trusted, while others, like Sea Shepherd Conservation Society, are young and edgy. How would you describe your non-profit if it were a person? Consider which corporates have a similar brand personality.

Values

The core values of a non-profit describe the heart of the organisation. They are not just the buzzwords that appear on brochures. Core values describe what the organisation stands for and could be things like inclusion, diversity, innovation and justice. Think about one or two values that describe your non-profit best and that infuse all of its programs, services and ethos. Identify the sort of corporate entities that demonstrate or aspire to similar values.

Assets and strengths

What does your non-profit do well? From the metrics and details in the asset catalogues, what strengths and main assets can it offer a corporate? For example, it could be your unique expertise, engaging content or niche audience. Identifying the strongest assets will enable the non-profit to identify who might be interested in those assets and how they represent an attractive proposition to a corporate partner.

Geographic footprint

COVID-19 saw a resurgence in corporates seeking to connect with the communities in which they operate. Giving and investing locally was seen as a way to demonstrate authentic commitment from businesses large and small. Your non-profit's geographic footprint will help to identify the businesses that operate in similar locations. It might be a national, state, metro or regional reach. Consider which businesses operate in similar locations or are expanding their business into new areas and might want to work with you.

Audiences - shared or desired

This is where the hard work in gathering metrics and details of your audiences pays off. It's difficult to get people's attention when social media, TV, mainstream media and other channels compete for space. By demonstrating clarity and proof of its audiences, followers and supporters, a non-profit can identify which corporates share a similar audience or have a desired audience. For example, the mental health charity Beyond Blue has a high brand awareness and a broad-based following in Australia. One of the hardest demographics for mental health services to reach is young males, who are less likely to seek help. Beyond Blue chose to partner with Steel Blue, manufacturers of work boots for trades people, to reach their predominantly male customer base.[5] The partnership enabled Steel Blue to connect with its customers in a way that demonstrated their genuine support for the audience's growing mental health issues.

Finding the right fit between audiences enhances the proposition for corporates and can fill much-needed gaps for either the corporate or the non-profit.

A shared interest in success

If your non-profit succeeds with its work, who else benefits? The New South Wales State Emergency Services (SES) has a major partnership with AAMI insurance.[6] The partnership encourages communities to proactively prepare for natural disasters and emergencies and builds community education and resilience. If households mitigate the impact of disasters, then SES will have fewer calls, AAMI will reduce their costs of insurance payouts and encourage more people to take up insurance. Which corporates might have a shared interest in your progress?

Within this area of synergy, it's worth considering the flipside of shared success. Which corporates are exacerbating the problem or perhaps unintentionally contributing to it? For example, Airbnb has been accused of contributing to the problem of homelessness by reducing the available rental housing stock.[7] Corporates may be unaware of the downstream impact of their activities and could be willing to explore a partnership that mitigates the effect or helps improve their business practices.

Core business and programs

A final area of potential synergy is in a non-profit's core business. For The Wilderness Society, it's the natural environment. For Guide Dogs, it's people living with a disability. And for UNICEF, it's children. Consider the natural area of common ground where a corporate has a similar focus. It's also useful to reflect on the areas identified in the risk management framework, to ensure that choices of prospective partners are perceived to be a good fit by a corporate and non-profit's key customers and stakeholders. The Smith Family is a well-respected Australia charity working to improve education for disadvantaged children. It proposed a partnership with BAE Systems, a global engineering company.[8] Unfortunately, BAE also manufactures armaments worldwide. Weapons and children aren't a natural fit and the partnership was concluded amid some adverse publicity.

By working through the four-step FIND process, a non-profit can refine, filter and make active choices about prospective corporate partners. It will be able to answer those key corporate questions: Where are you going? What do you need? Why me? Why now?

This method will ensure a thoughtful and strategic approach to choosing the right fit corporate partners. A non-profit will build the confidence of its leadership, board and staff by clearly articulating its choices and rationale. Some non-profits have taken this a step further and made their thinking publicly available to future corporate partners. A great example is the ethical charter of the Sydney Gay and Lesbian Mardi Gras, which sets out their principles, their expectations of partners and how choices are made.[9]

> Accidental brilliance is not a prospecting strategy.

Accidental brilliance is not a prospecting strategy. Moving from an ad hoc approach will save a non-profit months or years of time and effort and avoid the inevitable staff frustration and burnout. The proposition will be more compelling for a corporate and set the foundations for more sustainable partnership opportunities.

Partnerships require a proactive approach

Do you love bedtime stories? It was the favourite time of day when the kids were young, and we shared lots of picture book adventures. But the same old stereotypes persisted

– the beautiful princess waited passively in the tower for a handsome prince to rescue her and live happily ever after. Then there was *The Paper Bag Princess*. For those who haven't enjoyed this wonderful book, Princess Elizabeth is engaged to marry Prince Roland, but a dragon attacks the castle, burns all her clothes and kidnaps Roland. Dressed only in a paper bag, Elizabeth hunts and defeats the dragon and rescues Roland. Finally, a heroine for modern times!

The trope of the princess in the tower bears uncanny similarities to how many charities approach corporate partnerships. The approach is passive, timid and a little fearful. It's time to shake off the stereotypes and channel your inner Paper Bag Princess.

Rescue yourself

Proactively targeting corporate partners, based on synergies with your mission, values and mutual strategic priorities will put you in the driving seat for the best fit partners. Rapunzel was happy to wait until someone found her, but you're competing with thousands of other non-profits for the attention of a Prince Charming. A carefully selected shortlist of prospects, plus warm introductions from your network will yield better results than multiple cold proposals to an info@corporate.com inbox or a bigger Donate button on your website. Be bold and go after the partners you want – they're likely to need rescuing more than you.

Understand the value you bring

Do you want a corporate partner to see you as desperate and needy or as a valuable partner in an important enterprise? Your non-profit will probably be full of subject matter experts and passionate people working to solve some of society's thorniest and most important issues. Yes, you'd love to have more cash, time or resources, but you bring valuable expertise, audiences, brand trust and reputation to a partnership. You can help to advance the corporate's strategic objectives through the partnership and together you can make a real social impact. Non-profits build their confidence by clearly understanding their needs, assets and the value they have to offer a partner. This will be an equal marriage where you both slay the dragon together.

Choose which frog to kiss

Sometimes, a frog is really just a small, warty amphibian, not a handsome prince in disguise. When charities receive unsolicited approaches from corporates, it seems like their inner princess takes over. The faint promise of something exciting often leads them to make reactive decisions on partnerships without a realistic view of whether this is a frog or a prince. Gaining internal agreement on your no-go areas and putting in place a risk and decision-making framework will allow you to critically review every opportunity against criteria that are important to your charity. Then you'll have greater clarity and confidence about making the right decision on a partnership and won't be tempted to say Yes! to every passing frog with a twinkle in his eye.

> Channel your own internal dragon slayer and be bold.

For all non-profits looking for corporate partners, we recommend that you channel your own internal dragon slayer and be bold. Be confident and make your own decisions. Otherwise, you'll be waiting a long time in the tower.

CASE STUDY
Australian Ballet and Chanel

The Australian Ballet is the largest classical dance company in Australia. For over 60 years, it has inspired, challenged and delighted audiences with its many performances. COVID-19 saw its dancers limbering up in their lounge rooms as performances ceased during extended lockdowns. When The Australian Ballet team searched for new corporate partners, you would expect that they'd simply seek new income to fill the revenue black hole created by no ticket sales during COVID.

Instead, the team took a strategic approach and sought corporates that could help with the organisation's long-term mission. Chanel is a French luxury fashion house that has its own long association with ballet and performing arts. Chanel's core values were focused on preserving cultural heritage. The partnership with The Australian Ballet brought Chanel's expertise and substantial financial commitment to digitise and preserve the Ballet's archival film footage, photographs, costumes and history.[10] Creating a digital asset management system ensures The Australian Ballet's heritage is protected for future generations. It also created a valuable source of digital content that can be monetised and leveraged creatively. The partnership is a perfect alignment of values, core mission and skills, and creates value for both parties.

The Australian Ballet team went far beyond the traditional arts sponsorship approach of selling performances and advertising. It has secured decades of heritage and created assets that can be leveraged for years to come.

Conclusion

The path to successful corporate partnerships starts with some internal reflection. It's tempting to respond to the demands to 'just get out there' and find corporate partners. But if you don't know where 'there' is and what you need, you can spend a lot of time wandering in circles. Make sure you're confident about the answers to the key questions a corporate will ask: Where are you going? What do you need? Why me? Why now? If you can answer these for each prospect on your shortlist, you'll have a strong proposition for a partnership and be on the right path to success.

4

WIN New Partners

In Chapter Three, we focused on understanding your organisation to build the foundations for a strong value proposition and choosing the right partners. This chapter shifts from an internal to an external focus. How can you engage with corporates and inspire them about the opportunity to work together?

You've done the thinking and got a shortlist of corporate prospects that might be a good fit for your organisation. Now, you have to reach out to them. For many people in non-profits, the prospect can be daunting, even terrifying. It's like stepping into an unknown country where you don't speak the language. When our neighbour had a university essay due, she would always head to the kitchen and start baking; anything to delay the reality of a difficult task. We all have ways of confronting something difficult that typically falls under three responses.

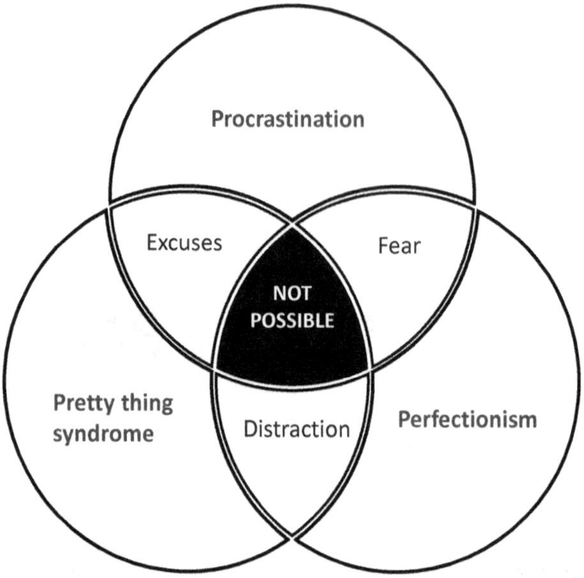

Figure 6: Strategies for delay and avoidance

Procrastination and perfectionism are close bedfellows; they're typically born of fear about the task ahead. Endlessly tweaking a proposal or approach creates delays and puts off the moment you're actually going to have to make that call. The author Elizabeth Gilbert says perfectionism is 'just fear dressed up in high heels and a mink coat, pretending to be fancy'.[1]

Fear can also make it easier to be distracted by the next pretty, shiny thing. Perhaps it's an exciting new piece of research, or maybe it's something mundane and ordinary. I've sometimes been excited by cleaning the oven rather than finishing a tricky report. Finding pretty shiny things to focus on gives plenty of excuses to procrastinate. Then you find that you haven't approached any corporates and your targets for the year look scary.

You can avoid sabotaging your success by building your skills and using easy tools and processes to make prospecting for corporate partners less of a mountain to climb. Using them regularly will increase your confidence and make those partnership approaches less terrifying. You have the opportunity to create a partnership that will transform your mission and your cause. Put aside procrastination and perfectionism and get started on prospecting.

The secret ingredient for success

In order to win new corporate partners, step into your prospect's shoes. It's not about you, it's about *them*.

How often have you attended a dinner party where your nearest neighbour talks about themselves all night without asking you a single question? Perhaps you were thrilled to know more about changes to accounting rules, the offside rule in soccer or the mating habits of barn owls. Or maybe you were bored and frustrated because your fellow diner seemed more interested in themselves than in you. For many corporates, it can feel just like that when they receive unsolicited approaches from non-profits. They get a cookie-cutter document that talks about the non-profit, its programs and its achievements. There's nothing personalised and it doesn't address any of the company's values, priorities or needs.

Heads up: you are *not* the hero of the story. Your non-profit is simply the catalyst for achieving solutions to their business problems and making a positive impact on the world. To win new partners, you must get under the skin of the corporate prospect and find out what matters most to them.

The single most important ingredient for winning partners is finding out the corporate's pain points and priorities.

Seek to understand the perspective of a corporate prospect and demonstrate that you understand what matters to them. Corporates are responsible to their shareholders, investors, staff and customers for their choices about where to invest their time and effort. If you can't show how a partnership with your non-profit will create real outcomes for their business objectives, not just your organisation or cause, you'll struggle to get their attention. You're competing with thousands of other registered non-profits, so find a way to stand out. If you have uncovered their pain points and priorities and can position yourself as part of the solution, you'll be miles ahead of any other non-profit.

_____

Find a way to stand out.

_____

Shaking off old habits

Do you remember the careers stand for corporate partnership managers at your university jobs fair? No, we don't either because it has never existed. People come into corporate partnerships with a range of different backgrounds, sometimes from sales or business development roles in the private sector. That means they start with a list of prospects and are keen to pick up the phone and get hustling. But you don't have tangible products and services to offer; you're selling hope. Hope for climate action, an end to poverty, a cure for a disease. A better world. Their default is to sell programs as their product, with limited success.

Others have marketing and advertising backgrounds, and some move across from different roles within a non-profit and get promoted into corporate partnerships. They struggle with the leap into acquisition and are stuck in the mindset that partnerships are the same as fundraising.

Partnership managers bring different skills and experiences that are undoubtedly useful. However, they must shake off some old habits and embrace an approach that puts a corporate's needs and priorities at the forefront of winning partnerships.

Background	Default approach	Winning approach
Sales and business development	Create a product, program or package and sell hard.	Explore a corporate's needs and pain points and be open to co-creating a solution.
Marketing and advertising	Offer marketing assets, logos and social media posts as benefits in return for corporate donations.	Deliver great content for them to share across channels and inspire their audiences. Don't assume they're interested in your logo.
Philanthropy and community fundraising	Develop a case for support that talks about the cause and need.	Create a credentials document that entices a corporate with a strong commercial proposition.
Event management	Run a gala ball and invite corporates to buy tickets or sponsorship.	Host intimate boardroom events that showcase your expertise and impact.
Program or service specialist	Select a program with a glossy report and images. Ask corporates to fund the program.	Use the program as a proof point of your ability to deliver impact. Explore a full range of partnership activations and value.

The traditional approach to partnerships has been very linear and is driven by the needs and perspectives of the non-profit. It follows like this:

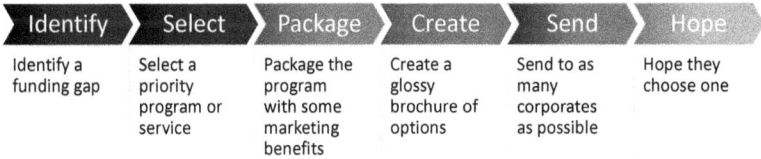

Identify	Select	Package	Create	Send	Hope
Identify a funding gap	Select a priority program or service	Package the program with some marketing benefits	Create a glossy brochure of options	Send to as many corporates as possible	Hope they choose one

Figure 7: Traditional linear approach to partnerships

Rinse and repeat until someone wonders why they're getting no results or they have a portfolio of low-value, highly demanding transactional partners.

The ideal approach requires non-profits to develop a deep understanding of the corporate's pain points, priorities and needs and invite them to collaborate on shaping the partnership. The process looks like this:

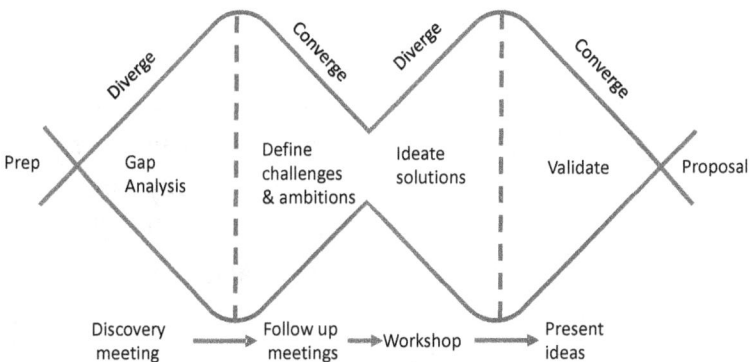

Figure 8: Collaborative approach to partnerships

At each point, there is an opportunity to develop deeper insights and test assumptions. It turns the prospective corporate partner into an active participant in the process, not the passive recipient of a ready-made proposal.

Preparation and research

Thorough preparation before making the first approach is super important. Do your homework before you're tempted to pick up the phone or hit send on that email. Failing to prepare is like turning up to a board meeting in your pyjamas and slippers. You won't make the right impression and you'll quickly feel under-dressed.

The point of preparation before any meeting or approach is to develop a hypothesis. Develop your own ideas of the corporate's pain points, ambitions and priorities so you can test them at the first and subsequent meetings. This will also help you frame your first approach so you lead with something that will pique their self-interest.

Conduct rigorous research on your corporate prospect. It will help you filter your shortlist and eliminate those who may have hidden issues of concern or are already committed to other non-profit partnerships in your sector. It will enable you to identify any areas of synergy or alignment with that corporate. Opposites don't attract in partnerships, so you're looking for things you have in common.

Things to look for when you research

Corporates like to present a curated and attractive public picture. It's no different from the social media influencers who post their glamorous outfits on Instagram. You won't see the messy closet, bad hair day or stretch marks.

A corporate rarely highlights its problems in reports or social media, so read between the lines. Be curious whilst reading any information and think about *why*. A healthy dose of curiosity and cynicism will help you decipher why they communicate the narrative you are reading.

Firstly, try to identify the hidden pain points for the business. For example, if a corporate lingers over its workplace awards, proclaiming that it's such a great place to work, what's the underlying problem? Perhaps it's staff attrition and low engagement scores. Are their staff suffering burnout or reluctant to return to the office after COVID? Another example of a pain point is market share; how are they performing compared with their competitors? Are they losing market share? Do they want to grow, but sales have been stagnant? Are they the market leader and want to retain their position?

Secondly, consider the pain points relevant to their industry sector. For example, the construction industry is currently experiencing skinny margins and a shortage of qualified workers. Governments are also requiring construction companies to meet gender equity targets if they want to tender for business. What are industry-wide pain points and how is your target corporate responding? Gaining insights into their industry sector will help you speak their language and create a common understanding.

Finally, consider what information you have gathered about the corporate's ambitions and strategic priorities. Do any of them align with your organisation's work? For example, if they are growing and expanding in new markets, are you already established in that geographic area or do you have the audiences they are looking for? Consider how your non-profit can help the corporate achieve their goals and ambitions.

You are researching your corporate prospect to develop a hypothesis about their current situation and identify where you can be part of the solution for their pain points and priorities. You are also gathering important information that will shape your initial questions and conversations.

Best sources of information

A wide range of information can be found through publicly available sources, enabling you to get a good picture of your corporate prospect. Try the following suggestions.

The company website and annual report

Obviously, you're getting the curated and polished version of facts they want to share. But you can identify apparent commonalities in their locations, activities, core business and typical audiences to see what you have in common.

Put on your sceptical and curious hat and consider the motivations behind the information the company chooses to highlight. If they talk about their exciting new brand refresh, you can guess they've got a problem with recognition and brand loyalty. Consider the example from the iconic Australian company Vegemite, which sells Australia's favourite spread.[2] Their website has an enormous range of branded merchandise, from socks to dog sweaters. This mass market approach suggests they're looking for increased brand reach and awareness. They have also listed recipes using Vegemite in non-traditional ways, including nachos, noodles and macaroni. They are clearly appealing to a new and more diverse audience for their product. The items in their annual report and website are important to that corporate. Think about how your non-profit helps them with those business priorities.

Recent press releases

It's illuminating to see the type of issues corporates choose to share with a wider audience through the company's annual report or corporate social responsibility report. The mining giant BHP has emphasised renewable energy initiatives to amplify its environmental credentials rather than its ongoing extractive activities.[3] BHP obviously wants to position the organisation as part of the solution for climate change rather than the problem.

Social media

Review the company's activity on social media platforms like LinkedIn, Facebook and X (formerly known as Twitter). Take a look at 12 months of activity, as it can provide valuable clues about seasonal fluctuations in their business. Think about how they talk about themselves and the issues that appear regularly. As with their annual report or website, you can get hints of the challenges they are facing.

A company may also celebrate its work with other non-profits through formal partnerships or ad hoc volunteering. Look at the emerging themes to see whether there are gaps in the portfolio that your non-profit could fill. Check if they are currently working with a non-profit competitor.

Notice the level of engagement with their posts. Companies often struggle to get good attention because their content is not particularly exciting. A partnership with your organisation can provide inspiration and interest for their audiences. Read through the comments on their posts; customers, suppliers or staff can be brutally honest on social media and hint at the challenges beneath the surface. Set up Google alerts to monitor the companies you're targeting so you won't miss any useful nuggets of information.

Competitors

Consider your prospect's main competitors and their relative positioning. If you have a specific target in mind, see if you can tap into your networks to interview one of their competitors.

I once investigated a partnership opportunity with the high-street retailer Specsavers by asking for insight from a contact at OPSM, a direct competitor. OPSM were very happy to offer broad insights into the challenges faced by their sector and offered some juicy information about their competitor's challenges, key people and customers. That insight helped shape the partnership proposition and get straight to the decision-makers.

LexisNexis

This is a powerful online business, news and legal research database. LexisNexis provides access to billions of public records globally, from legal cases to news releases. It is the best site if you want to unearth a company's legal skeletons or issues that are bubbling below the surface. The downside is that it's incredibly expensive, so we don't recommend buying access. If you have a volunteer or intern from a law firm, they can access it for you from their business account.

Your own database

Have you checked your own CRM to see how many donors have an @yourprospectname.com email address? Have you searched whether the CEO, chair or other senior executives already give to your cause?

We were once surprised to receive a phone call from an EA to the CEO of one the world's largest mining companies about a donation. The company was a prospect on our list, yet we hadn't even searched for his name on our regular donor list. He had been giving to the charity for five years!

Developing your partnership hypothesis

Your partnership hypothesis is a summary of what you suspect are the main priorities, ambitions and pain points of your corporate prospect. Remember, this is only a hypothesis and will be tested when you conduct a discovery meeting, but it's an important precursor to making the first approach.

Do this by drawing up two tables. In the first, list what you believe are their pain points in one column and possible solutions in another.

In the second table, make a list of their main ambitions, based on your research about their strategy. In the second column, list how a partnership with you will help them to achieve their ambitions.

An example might look like this:

ABC Clothing Retailer

Pain points	Solutions
Declining market share	Authentic engagement with their core audience
Customer complaints on social media	Inspiring and emotional new content for their social channels
Decreasing store traffic	In-store activations that drive footfall

Pain points	Solutions
Constant advertising for new staff	Enhancing their employee value proposition. Access to new untapped workforce through NFP employment pathways program.
Struggling with environmental impact of fast fashion	Recycle and rehome excess stock through donations to community beneficiaries

Strategic ambitions	Solutions
Launching a brand refresh	Reinvigorate brand positioning through social purpose and community partnership
Growing their online reach	Joint campaigns to shared audiences, using NFP's reach and content
Re-engaging with their core female audience	Investment in programs that directly impact and benefit their target customers

What do you have in common with your prospect?

Why is this prospect the ideal partner for you?

What can they provide to further your mission that no other business can?

Your hypothesis should start to answer the Why Me? question outlined in Chapter Three. Your approach should demonstrate why you've chosen this corporate for a partnership out of thousands of other registered businesses. Importantly, you've spent time getting into the head of your corporate prospect. It will ensure that your first approach is all about them and confirm that a partnership with you is worth the investment. It's very different to the traditional fundraising approach to partnerships.

Preparation and developing a hypothesis before you embark on the first meeting is vital to ensure you don't fall into the trap of that one-sided conversation. Show that you've taken the time to understand your corporate prospect's industry, environment and business and you'll have a much stronger proposition for your partner.

Getting the first meeting

The preparation is done, your research has given useful insights and you have a shortlist of your best prospects.

Now, the challenge is to get the first meeting to test your hypothesis and explore partnership possibilities. Note that the emphasis is on a *meeting*, not sending out a mass email to info@corporate.com and hoping that someone responds. You'll be wasting your time on the latter.

Your approach to getting the meeting depends on whether you have a warm introduction or if it's a cold contact. Ideally, you'll have reached out to your networks using the connections identified through your research. You may even be able to leverage the contacts of your non-profit's leadership, board or ambassadors.

Figure 9: Getting the first meeting

If you have a warm contact, you can ask directly for a meeting. If you have no contacts at the corporate prospect, getting to the most relevant person may take a few steps. Create a teaser to get their attention before you make the email or phone approach.

The wonderful partnership manager at Sydney Children's Hospitals Foundation sent her prospects a tea bag with the message, 'You and me and a cup of tea?'. For Save the Children UK's Christmas Jumper campaign, Sharon's mum produced tiny, knitted jumpers that were sent to prospects as a teaser about the campaign.[4]

A teaser is useful for getting attention and warming up a cold prospect for your first approach.

Rules for the first approach

Whether you're making the first approach by phone or email, the overriding principle is the same. *It's all about them*. Make it relevant to their business and give them a reason to respond. That's why you do your preparation beforehand. The other key rules are:

1. Don't try to sell. The objective of the first approach is to get the meeting, not to sell a partnership. Don't try to sell them something before you've even met them.

2. Name drop. If you have a warm introduction, make sure you include the name. It creates a sense of obligation to that shared connection and enhances your credibility.

3. Be succinct. No one has time to read a biography of your organisation, and it's not really about you, remember? You want to pique their interest, not send them to sleep.

4. A gallon of self-interest and a teaspoon of inspiration. This is the closest thing to a formula for success in the first approach. Read your script or your email and make sure you've got the right balance. It has to be focused heavily on the corporate's priorities, with just a sprinkle of

something interesting about your non-profit and your work. Give your corporate prospect a reason to respond.

5. Fifteen seconds. That's the typical time a corporate prospect will take to consider whether they'll respond to your approach, pass it on to someone relevant or hit the delete button. Corporates have busy people with full inboxes and lots of calls. You've only got a short window to get their attention.

When you're preparing your initial call or email, use the principles developed by sales and speakership guru Col Fink.[5] Make it a SPEAR approach, not a LINEAR approach:

Short, **P**ersonal, **E**xpecting **A** **R**esponse

not

Long, **I**mpersonal, **N**ot **E**xpecting **A** **R**esponse

Here are some examples to show you the difference.

SPEAR email:

Dear Jo,

Anna Chen suggested you as ABC Corp's expert in social responsibility. Congrats on your recent award for the Best Place to Work. Did you know that one in three of your employees will experience poor mental health in the next year? I'd like to talk to you about our work to improve mental health and wellbeing, and how it can increase workforce performance and engagement in your teams. I'm available next Tuesday and Wednesday for a meeting. Would either of those work for you?

Regards,

Jay Murphy

LINEAR email:

Dear Jo,

Great Minds Australia is a well-respected non-profit founded in 1953 by the visionary John Smith in the outback town of Leonora, WA. Our mission is to improve the health and wellbeing of Australians by creating a variety of programs that enable empowerment, education, research and community participation.

We are celebrating our 70th anniversary this year and have a range of events planned, including a gala ball, community fun run and online trivia quiz. I attach a brochure outlining the events and the sponsorship packages available.

If you'd like to support this very important cause, please email your interest to events@greatminds.com.

Thank you for your consideration.

Jay Murphy

You can see the differences and which plays most significantly to the self-interest of the corporate prospect. Which one would you prefer to receive?

At the first meeting

Before you get into the room or hop onto that video conference, make sure you have a meeting plan. Partnership managers will need to adapt as the meeting progresses, but it makes things much easier if you have a plan first. This is particularly important if you're bringing someone to the meeting with you. You want to be clear on each person's role and not trip over each other. A meeting plan could be a simple one-page document and should include the following:

Who are you meeting?	What do you know about them? Where are the areas to build rapport?
Which areas of your research do you want to investigate?	Where would you like to steer the conversation? What challenges do you think the company and their industry face?
Why are you meeting?	What's your hypothesis for a partnership? What's relevant to the person you're meeting?
What objections do you foresee?	What are the barriers that might prevent the next step? How can you overcome them?
What's your ideal next step?	Is it a further meeting? Or introduction to someone more senior or more relevant? How will you secure it?

A meeting plan will help things go smoothly and you won't look uncoordinated in front of your corporate prospect.

Importantly, you'll be able to guide the conversation forward to the next meeting or next step.

The discovery meeting

During this first meeting, your main objective is to extract as much information from your prospect as possible. It feels counter-intuitive; you've got the first meeting and you can't wait to share everything you know about your cause, your organisation and how you can change the world. But you won't land a partnership with one meeting. You need a lot more information to test your hypothesis and decide what kind of partnership will work for both organisations. Instead of launching into a sales pitch, ask plenty of questions.

> You won't land a partnership with one meeting.

Remember the success of your final proposal will be determined by the information you gather during your first and subsequent meetings. It's not the closing comments that count; it's the quality of discovery at the start.

A common trap for partnership managers is to create wonderful rapport with the corporate prospect but forget to ask the key questions that will help you shape your partnership response. The meeting flew by, and you know everything about their family, favourite sports team and pets, but you haven't advanced your knowledge about their business. To make things easier, we've created an easy DISCOVERY question template to make sure nothing important is missed.

D	Decision maker	Are you speaking to the right person? Who will have the final decision or approval rights for a partnership? Who else should be involved in this conversation?
I	Important	What's important to them? Main priorities, business drivers, community interests?
S	Squeaky wheel	What's the organisation's biggest challenge? Why? How can a partnership help?
C	Capacity	What is their budget and appetite? What financial year do they operate on? Do they have budget allocated for community partnerships?
O	Other partners	Who else do they have relationships with? Any conflicts of interest? Previous experience (good or bad) with other organisations?
V	Values	What are they? Are the organisational culture and values a good fit?
E	External factors	What could influence them or a partnership? Is anything changing in the competitive environment? Any external pressures from customers, suppliers, regulators or government?
R	Risk appetite	Find out about their risk appetite and any potential conflict areas. What do they perceive as controversial causes or issues?
Y	You	Find out about the main contact, their interests, likes and dislikes. How do they like to be contacted, e.g. text, email, phone.

While you'll be asking a lot of questions and trying to find areas of opportunity and juicy insights, beware of making it feel like an interrogation. Be interested and curious, not dominating or aggressive. Plenty of open questions like 'Why?' or 'Tell me more about that' will genuinely demonstrate your interest.

Your corporate prospect may never have heard of your organisation, or you might have good brand recognition with little understanding beneath the headline. Give a brief precis, but don't fall into the trap of giving your prospect an entire biography. Instead, you want to insert some golden nuggets into the conversation. What are golden nuggets?

These are key pieces of information from your area of expertise that you can insert into the conversation. It could be something that:

- impacts their business operations
- impacts their staff
- is a pressing societal issue
- is now more urgent than ever
- is an emerging, hidden issue
- is heart-warming or inspiring
- changes the way they see the world.

What can you use to surprise, inspire or make them think? Prepare a treasure trove of these gold nuggets in advance to use in future corporate conversations. They could be statistics, recent research (your own or publicly available) or human stories. Use them sparingly during the first meeting to grab the corporate's interest and leave them with something memorable. You can bet that a well-chosen story or little-known fact will be the one they share with a colleague or boss after the meeting, and they'll remember it for longer.

Some great examples:

- 45% of Australians will experience a mental health condition in their lifetime and eight lives are lost to suicide every day. (Beyond Blue)
- Australians consume the equivalent of a fishbowl (or 3.8 litres) of pure alcohol every year. Unproductive workers with hangovers cost the Australian economy a staggering $26 billion every year. (febfast)
- Medical advances mean that we have the potential to eliminate cervical cancer by 2030. (Cancer Council)
- The national gender pay gap is 14.1%, meaning that women work two months more than men every year to earn the same amount. (Workplace Gender Equality Agency)

Demonstrate your knowledge and expertise in a way that builds your credibility as a partner and shows that you have something to offer.

The second (or third or fourth!) meeting

A partnership isn't built in a day and will certainly take more than one meeting. There will be many further meetings and discussions with your prospective corporate partner.

Use these meetings to test and refine the information you've gathered so far. Are you clear on their needs, priorities and pain points? Who else from your non-profit could you bring to advance the discussion, such as a specialist expert, CEO, or ambassador? Are there key decision-makers or stakeholders that the corporate prospect needs to include?

As the discussions progress, introduce potential solutions to the issues you have identified. During those meetings, open the door to a possible collaboration. It's less about what you can do, or what your corporate prospect should do; it's an invitation to collaborate on achieving great outcomes together.

The path to a final proposal or pitch isn't linear. There will be opportunities to expand thinking and then get more focus. Inviting your corporate prospect to collaborate on creating solutions and shaping the partnership will get you more commitment and usually better outcomes. By the time you reach the final proposal, it will become a summation of all your discussions and much easier to get the final Yes.

The 5Ps of pitching and proposals

Once you've built a rapport with your corporate prospect and the discussions have started to uncover the possibilities of working together, you may be asked to conduct a formal pitch or proposal. This will be the culmination of all your discussions, research and discovery.

There's no miracle script for a successful pitch, no matter what sales gurus may tell you. Proposals for corporate partnerships are won or lost on the information you've gathered along the way and how you've responded to what's

> There's no miracle script for a successful pitch.

important to the corporate. However, five key elements will help you structure a compelling pitch.

1. Planning and preparation

Be ready within your organisation before you make an external pitch to a corporate. The good news is that you'll have everything in place if you have identified what you need from a partner, the assets you can offer and your value proposition. The rest comes from your desktop research about your partner and the information you've gleaned from multiple meetings.

2. Perspective

Consider the corporate's perspective and ensure you've addressed their pain points, hopes and aspirations. Your corporate prospect should instantly recognise why they should partner with you and how your proposal is relevant to their business priorities and ambitions. Honour your partner by showing that you've listened to what's important to them and created solutions rather than leading with your needs or your funding gap.

3. Partnership profile

Don't make your corporate partner do all the work. Outline how the partnership will be structured and advanced. Paint a picture of the future, including:

How will the business be involved? e.g. skills, resources, funds, networks, expertise

Who will be managing the partnership?

How sustainable will this be?

What does success look like for both partners?

What's the outcome or impact of the partnership?

Corporate partners want to understand the key aspects of the partnership so they can assess the implications for their business. Your final pitch or proposal will normally cross the desk of the chief financial officer or the person authorising the budget commitment. It needs to include enough specifics for the left-brain people to be comfortable.

4. Proof

If you're proposing a significant partnership, give the corporate some comfort that you're a credible partner. That includes testimonials or case studies of previous successful partnerships, tangible evidence of outcomes, success stories or highlights. Create an 'evidence bank' from other partnerships to draw upon for future pitches.

Importantly, demonstrate the social outcomes achieved *and* the business results for your corporate partner. That might include increased staff engagement, positive PR, increased sales or better brand awareness. You won't be able to measure this yourself. Ask existing or previous partners to provide that information. Get smart and build it into future partnership contracts to ensure you have the necessary insights. If this is your first corporate partnership, use testimonials from significant donors or public research on the impact of a similar partnership, for example, cause marketing.

5. Panache

The final P is panache or pizzazz. Partnerships are a mixture of heart and science, so ensure your pitch is emotionally engaging, not just rational. Appeal to the marketing creatives, not just the CFO. Think about how to bring your pitch to life and don't just offer death by PowerPoint or long Word documents. In other words, pimp your pitch. Here are some examples of ways in which creative non-profits have engaged their audience:

- Use props. People love to play with physical things as they stimulate memory recall. An international aid agency measured out the items in an emergency ration pack and displayed them in containers on the boardroom table. Participants could touch and feel the items for themselves.
- Use experiences. A theatre company working with disabled performers brought blindfolds for the corporate audience to mimic the experience of

their performers. Another children's charity used virtual reality headsets to demonstrate the life of a community in an overseas program and 'walk' the audience through their village.

- Use people. A cancer charity brought a young survivor to tell her story from diagnosis to remission and relate to the audience on a personal level. A ballet company cleverly brought an existing corporate partner to talk about the great outcomes their partnership had achieved for their own company.

Engage the head and the heart in your pitch or proposal. Non-profits are usually excellent storytellers with an abundance of content, so there is plenty of opportunity to leave your corporate prospect with a memorable experience.

Pricing and how much to ask for

This is literally the million-dollar question. You don't want to feel like you've underdone the opportunity, but maybe you're fearful of offending your corporate prospect by asking for too much. In the same way that selling feels a bit distasteful, people generally hate asking for money. They prioritise approval and avoid a robust negotiation. Non-profits often revert to pricing tiers or packages to get around the tough discussion. Offering a ready-

Think like an airline; they are the evil geniuses of pricing.

made suite of gold, silver and bronze benefits and asking the corporate to pick one is a conflict avoidance strategy, not a way to maximise value.

Reframing the ask around the value you're offering and the amazing solutions you bring to a corporate's problems will help you be braver about pricing. You've done the

> There is no single price for everyone.

hard work on your assets and what you bring to the table. Now think about value through the eyes of your prospect, not your own non-profit.

Think like an airline; they are the evil geniuses of pricing.

How? Firstly, they know so much about us. They know you'll buy economy class if you're travelling on a family holiday, but your employer might pay for business if you're working. They know you prefer an aisle seat or a vegetarian meal. They gain so much data they can predict your price tolerance.

Secondly, airlines will present you with different choices within the price. Would you like a hire car, accommodation or a side trip with your flight? How about priority booking or extra luggage? They are adding value to justify a higher price.

Finally, the most important thing of all: *there is no single price for everyone.* The price of a flight that gets you home on Christmas Eve is not the same as one in mid-September. What looks like good value for a business traveller may seem exorbitant for a backpacking student.

Pricing is less of a science and more of an art, mixed with a dose of courage. To unpack the potential ask for a corporate, consider the following elements.

The corporate's appetite and budget: Is this a one-off campaign or part of a longer relationship? What budget do they have available this year? If they want to start small, can you plan an increase over the coming years?

Timing and urgency: Is there an external factor driving immediate action? Is there pressure due to an external pain point or community expectation such as bushfires, natural disasters or bad PR.

Substitution costs: Could the corporate get what you're offering elsewhere? It might be access to a target audience, specialist expertise or geographic footprint. What would it cost them if the corporate could access these assets and benefits alone, or in a commercial arrangement? For example, one corporate spent millions creating video animations to inspire families with children to buy their toothpaste. The campaign flopped. Then a non-profit proposed a partnership that would showcase the product with their established audience of exactly the target demographic. It was a bargain for the corporate, who committed $200,000 (not millions) to get the outcome they wanted.

Value: What pain point or hot spot does this partnership address? How much has the corporate already spent on trying to fix it? What does the corporate find valuable or hard to find? For example, high staff turnover and a reluctance to return to working in the office was costing one corporate millions of dollars. Their brand new retail park was struggling. A non-profit working in the same area was able to offer team engagement opportunities that provided a catalyst for bringing staff together and back into the office.

Cost of inaction: If the corporate doesn't choose a partnership with you and does nothing, how much will they lose? What are the costs of inaction on staff engagement, customer acquisition or lost sales? If you can show that the corporate will be worse off without your partnership, you'll have a very strong proposition.

Value is subjective, so pricing needs to be adaptive. What's a highly desirable set of Jimmy Choo heels for one person might be kryptonite for someone who loves sneakers. You think your snow boots are worth millions, but if you're selling them in Hawaii in the summer, you won't find a buyer. Think like an airline and understand your corporate partner's view of value. You'll have a clearer picture of the right price for your partnership and more confidence in making the ask.

Dealing with objections

If you've crafted your pitch or proposal well and addressed the corporate's hot spots and pain points, you should be well prepared to deal with objections. There may be a new decision maker at the table, or something might have shifted within the corporate's business for them to seek clarification or raise questions.

Objections can simply be a way for the corporate to seek more information. The best approach is to follow the LAARC approach: Listen, Acknowledge, Assess, Respond, Confirm. Be open and curious about their question. Acknowledging and repeating their objection helps you clarify the real issue and buys thinking time to craft your response. Ask some follow-up 'Why' questions of your own. Don't see objections as a massive hurdle. They're often a positive signal of interest as the corporate is asking for more information.

> Objections can simply be a way for the corporate to seek more information.

Many objections or negative responses are not actually a No. You have the opportunity to reposition many objections and turn them into opportunities.

If you've done a thorough job with your discovery meetings by asking the right questions and continually checking in with your prospect during the process, you should be well-positioned to deal with any issues long before the final pitch. Unless something has radically changed for your corporate, like a new CEO or a business crisis, you should expect a positive response at this stage.

If you don't get approval to proceed, leave them with a positive impression and keep the door open to future opportunities. One education non-profit reported that previous corporate prospects that had gone cold, reappeared during the early phases of COVID lockdowns and wanted to re-engage. They now had a clear impetus for a partnership where they couldn't see it before. They came back to the non-profit because they'd had such a great experience of dealing with them and were now ready for a partnership. Be aware of the impression you leave behind.

Most often, your preparation, research and relationship management will put you in a strong position for a final Yes from your corporate partner. You're on your way to building a sustainable and significant corporate partnership.

CASE STUDY
Legacy Australia

Legacy Australia provides essential support to the families of veterans, ensuring that no one suffers as a result of their loved one's service to the country. In 2023, Legacy celebrated its centennial, a significant milestone. But during recent years, the Legacy name has become less well known. Other causes have been more prominent and new organisations are working in innovative ways to support veterans. Legacy created the Centenary Torch Relay as a catalyst to reinvigorate the brand, inspire the community and position itself for the next 100 years.[6] The biggest problem was starting from scratch with no corporate partners.

Legacy followed the strategic process outlined in this book, building a clear idea of their needs, value proposition and offer. This allowed them to target the best fit corporate prospects and use their limited time wisely. The Legacy team were ambitious in the level of support they requested from corporate partners, confident with their offering and avoided the trap of the gold, silver and bronze sponsorship approach used in previous years.

Within 12 months, Legacy had secured three key partners, Defence Health, BAE and Lockheed Martin, yielding over AU$5 million in support. In addition, they received in-kind commitments of over AU$6.5 million from other key partners. The prospecting isn't finished yet and the Legacy team are confident they'll hit their desired target of AU$10 million in support. They will have gone from zero to hero in less than 18 months. Most importantly, bringing together the 44 Legacy clubs across Australia through the Torch Relay and its corporate partners has inspired members to collaborate more effectively and renew their pride in the organisation. The next 100 years are looking very bright for Legacy.

Conclusion

Winning corporate partners takes time, patience and resilience to keep going. But there's never been a better time to get started. The key to success is understanding that partnerships are all about them, not you.

Approaching corporates in the same way as you do with philanthropy, talking about your organisation's needs and programs will fall flat.

Offering a commercial proposition that solves a corporate's pain points and helps their ambitions will ensure a much warmer welcome for your approach. If you can demonstrate how your partnership saves or makes them money, it will quickly get the stamp of approval.

Doing your research, developing understanding and empathy for the corporate's needs and priorities and sprinkling your proposition with the non-profit magic of emotion and inspiration will guarantee a winning formula with new corporate partners.

GROW Exceptional Partners

Gardens can sometimes look like a wasteland. If you don't pay regular attention to the vegetable patch, the tomatoes become spindly and the herbs go to seed. It starts off looking lush and promising, but you get busy with other things and don't give it the regular attention it needs. By contrast, your grandmother's garden probably flourishes, with well-established shrubs and trees bearing fruit year after year. The major difference is in the amount of nurturing, focus and interventions when needed, not as a last resort.

Corporates know retaining existing customers is better than finding new ones. It's at least six times as expensive to acquire a new customer than to retain an existing one. A 5% increase in retention can increase revenue by at least 25%.[1] A continual focus on increasing annual revenue KPIs can sometimes divert attention away from the hidden value in existing relationships. At that stage, your list of previous partners starts to look longer than your list of current ones. There is some natural attrition in partnerships as corporates get bought out, finances fluctuate, or the leadership decides on a fresh direction. But the very best partnerships are built on relationships developed over time and nurtured by good gardeners.

Prioritise

In the busyness of a growing partnership portfolio, it can be tempting to spend more time on the most demanding partners at the expense of those with more potential. Like a classroom full of kids, it's often the noisiest or the naughtiest that grab the attention. There can also be favourites; the ones who are always a delight to call, who share your personal interests or who don't demand too much. You've got lots of plates to juggle, so make sure each gets the right level of attention.

Getting an objective view of your portfolio can be a challenge if you've managed them for a while. You can forget your original intentions for the partnership, or they may have veered off track. I recommend an annual review of your whole portfolio to see where you're spending your time and effort and which are yielding the best return.

The following is a prioritisation matrix to give you a fresh perspective.

		Alignment		
		Low	Mid	High
Engaged ↑ Relationship ↓ **Disengaged**	**High + peer to peer**	Reposition 3 Energy suckers but low value and little potential	Progress 6 Assess opportunities. Inspire and nurture to maintain or move to transformational	Transformational 9 Achieve social impact. Multiple partnership achievements
	Warm	Watch/Review 2 Be aware of how much time you spend on the partnership	Maintain 4 Nurture and maximise	Grow 6 Set partnership vision and goals. Get organisation buy in
	Cold	Harvest 1 Low account management just accept the money	Assess 2 Transactional relationship - limited impact	Actively nurture 3 Partnership at risk
		1 or 2 Pillars	3 Pillars	4+ Pillars
		Pillars of Activity		

Low Value ⟵————————————⟶ High Value

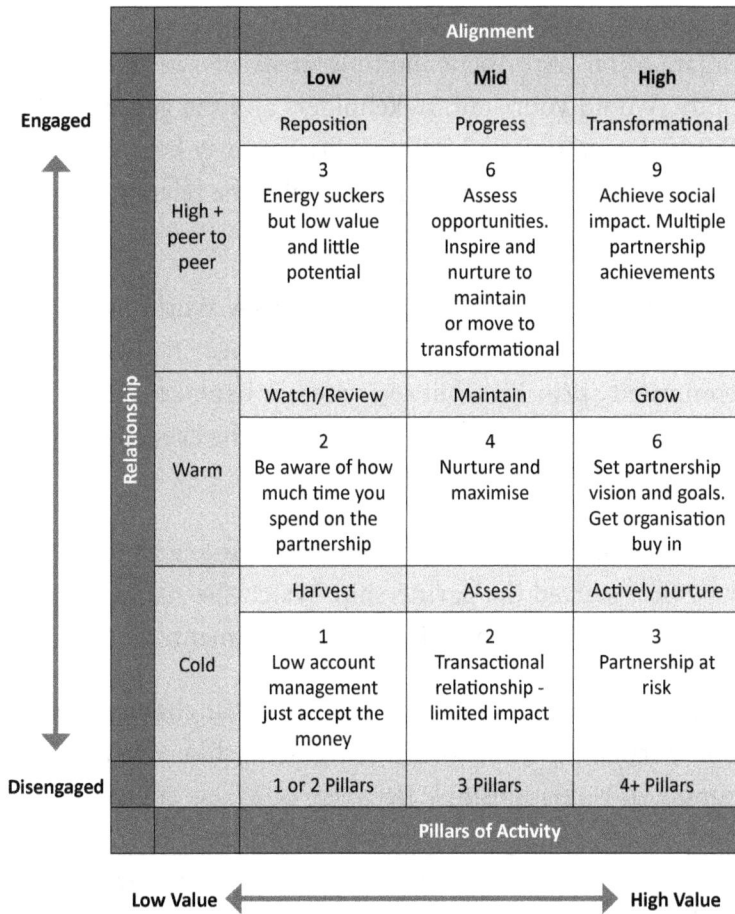

Figure 10: Prioritisation matrix

The three dimensions of relationship, alignment and pillars of activity assess the current state and future potential of each corporate partner. Each dimension contributes to the value of a partnership and helps build a realistic picture of the opportunity. Map your portfolio onto this matrix.

Alignment refers to the fit of the partner with your organisation. Are there multiple areas of synergy for you both? Would your staff, stakeholders and the general public think it's a natural and intuitive fit? You may have a valuable partner, but if the alignment isn't right, the relationship may not be sustainable.

A large bank chose to support the FINA World Swimming Championships. There was no obvious fit with their community priorities, but a very senior bank executive had a son in the Australian swim team. When the executive moved on, the partnership was not renewed.

Sooner or later, someone will scratch their head and wonder why they started the partnership. Watch the risk of attrition for a partner that doesn't have great alignment.

Relationships can start with an individual champion or in one particular area. To grow a partnership, don't rely on simple 1-1 relationships between one key contact and a partnership manager. The most valuable relationships are at multiple levels of each organisation. It inspires participation and commitment, becomes part of the company culture and makes it much harder for a partner to flip you for another organisation.

Pillars of activity refer to the range of value that you derive from the partnership. It may start with a transactional partnership, with the partner simply funding a program. That's great, but explore how to move it from transactional to more strategic. The greater the number of pillars of activity, the more entrenched and valuable the partnership.

Not every partner will be transformational and that's normal. Take a realistic view of each partner's value and potential and adjust your attention, resources and effort accordingly.

Take another look at the prioritisation matrix. For the partners in boxes 1-3, make a choice about whether to invest in the relationship. If you have only one or two pillars of activity and the relationship isn't particularly deep, but the partner is low maintenance and undemanding, bank the cheque knowing they don't want much in return. It's usually token corporate philanthropy, but it still adds to your bottom line if you don't expend too much effort.

Partners involved in three or more pillars of activity are more valuable, so explore why the relationship is still cold. The partnership may have been warm, but perhaps a key person has left, or the focus has changed. Some active relationship nurturing will be required to see if the partnership can be revived or retired.

The most frustrating partners are those who love your organisation and have great relationships with everyone, but give you very little. They're demanding and suck your time and energy. Be careful to moderate the attention they get for the value you receive. If you can't increase their value, decrease your focus and resourcing as these partners detract from time spent on more valuable opportunities.

The partners in boxes 4, 6 and 9 are your best performers and have the greatest potential. Focus your efforts here to grow or maintain the relationship. That's why you need to be ruthless with the underperformers or the energy suckers.

Create a portfolio plan for your partners that sets out the goals and ambitions for each one. Partners will move around this matrix over time, and it should trigger an appropriate response that might increase the amount of effort or decide that it's time to harvest and move on. An annual review of the portfolio will ensure that the focus is maintained on those with real growth potential.

Nurture

The weeds will reappear in your garden if you haven't been paying regular attention. It's the same with partnerships if you want them to grow and thrive, not wither through neglect. Getting to a Yes and signing the contract is the start, not the end point, for the partnership. Things can change quickly in the corporate landscape, so be alert and nimble to keep the partnership performing. Instead of the sales trope of 'always be closing', the better stance is 'always be opening', which constantly looks for new opportunities to grow and deepen the relationship.

Always be opening

Regular partnership reviews are essential. They can be formal six-monthly reviews or simply monthly or quarterly check-ins. They are an opportunity to get updates on what is changing in your corporate partner's world and see how that impacts the partnership. Don't get too bogged down in reporting activities; instead, ask if they are still meeting the overall partnership vision and objectives.

The most effective way of conducting partnership reviews is to imagine that your corporate partner is a brand-new prospect. When you've been in partnership for a while, it's like being in a long-standing marriage. At the beginning, you're intensely curious about each other and everything is a novelty. After a few years, you've got into a rhythm and you're sitting together on the sofa in your tracksuit, eating Doritos on a Saturday night. If you have an 'always be opening' mindset, you'll treat them like you're still on honeymoon. That means continually checking on their needs and looking for new ways to keep the partnership fresh. Think of partnership reviews as re-discovery sessions and you'll be looking forward, not back.

> Think of partnership reviews as re-discovery sessions.

You may be a great relationship manager, but are you prepared to challenge your corporate partner to think about their own business differently? We often encounter non-profits with a mature portfolio of partners that haven't grown significantly since the early years. It can feel awkward to dig deeper into their business when you've known them for a while. It's like asking questions when you've been in a job for a year and you think you should know it all by now. But the business environment is changing fast, and corporate CEOs are struggling to keep up with the demands of their staff and customers. 'Always be opening' or you'll fail to uncover what's new in their world and grow and adapt your partnership.

Measure and celebrate success

Make sure you agree on the measures of success in the partnership and celebrate the milestones. Your partnership vision may be audacious and ambitious, so mark smaller wins along the way. Give your corporate partner something they can share with their staff, customers and audiences to show that you're making progress. Don't make them wait until the end of the five-year contract to celebrate.

Equally, if they are achieving better business results from the partnership, make sure you're recording them. They will be proof points you can use for your next corporate prospect. If the partnership has helped them increase staff engagement, make more sales or win new business, that's important for you to know. You can celebrate what you've achieved for their business, not just community beneficiaries.

Don't forget to thank them

When was the last time you properly thanked your corporate partner? Did you invite them to a special event or give them a shout-out on social media? You don't have to send champagne to let them know that the relationship is valued. One organisation working with sick children got a few families to shoot raw, 60-second videos on their phones, talking about the impact of the partnership on their lives. It wasn't fancy or expensive, but heartfelt and authentic. Remember that your partners are human, so connect them emotionally to your cause.

Get your leadership involved

Involve the C-Suite in your organisation when you're thanking your partners or nurturing the relationship. It demonstrates the importance of the partnership to your organisation and builds connections at multiple levels. Individuals move on to new roles all the time, so ensure that your partnership isn't dependent on one person to sustain it. During COVID, this was particularly relevant for one charity whose main corporate partners were an airline, a hotel chain and a shopping centre. It sounded like a balanced portfolio until lockdowns hit, the businesses went into freefall and the key contacts were made redundant. Involving your leadership in developing peer to peer relationships not only strengthens the partnership but mitigates again key person risk.

Get your colleagues involved

Create an internal coalition of people from your organisation and the corporate partner. It really does take a village to win and sustain corporate partnerships. Involve people with different skills to deliver on the partnership, such as marketing, communications, PR, programs and services, volunteering and ambassadors. Building a working group or coalition that enables your key people to connect with those on the corporate side will prevent you from being the conduit for everything. It's like being stuck in the neck of an egg-timer; very tight, uncomfortable and ultimately an unproductive place for a relationship manager to be.

Move from this:

To this:

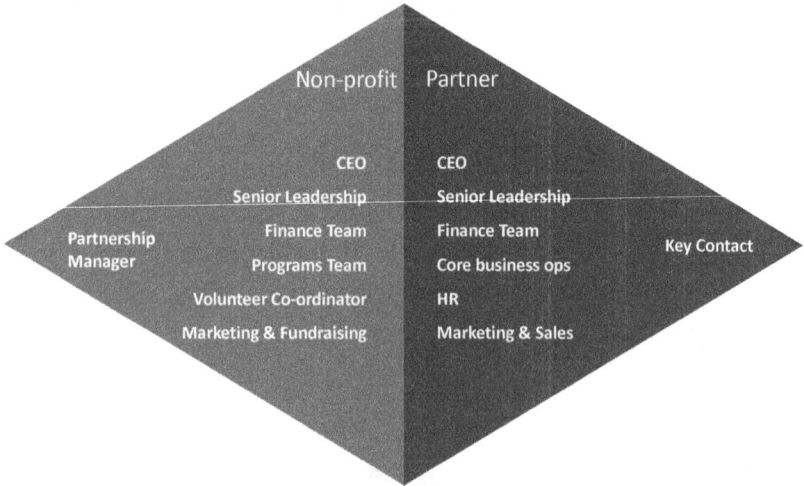

Figure 11: Old and new models of partnership

Remember the simple things

Some of the simplest things can help to nurture and grow a partnership. Try the following.

Invite your prospect to:

- a program/site visit to see your work in action or meet an expert
- any events that you are hosting
- launches, awards and celebration events.

Offer:

- to present at a lunch-and-learn to their staff or customers
- a conversation with a champion or an ambassador.

Share:

- latest research, content or a case study
- insights relevant to their industry or the core issues
- interim impact reports.

You've worked so hard to win that corporate partnership. Don't undermine all that work by neglecting the relationship after the contract is signed. Keep the garden flourishing and it will reward you for years to come.

Maximise value

You've identified your strongest opportunities and want to take the partnership from good to great. The partnership architecture in Figure 12 shows your starting point.

Figure 12: Partnership architecture

Non-profits typically spend a lot of time on *what* the partnership does at the expense of *why* the partnership exists in the first place. This is the result of narrow KPIs focused on raising income at the expense of greater value.

If you want to maximise the value of a relationship, elevate the thinking to create a partnership vision. Doing this in collaboration with your partner will inject ambition and aspiration into the partnership. You'll be able to set clear goals that will be your markers of success and milestones of progress. The partnership activities will be the proof points that deliver the overall vision rather than as an end in themselves. The 'What' will probably evolve and change over time, but the 'Why' will endure as the anchor point for the partnership.

When Tesco, the giant UK grocery retailer, partnered with the World Wildlife Fund (WWF), they set an ambitious vision to 'halve the environmental impact of the average UK shopping basket'.[2] Achieving this vision will ensure everyone can access affordable, healthy and sustainable food. This vision is supported by three main goals:

1. Helping everyone eat more sustainably.
2. Restoring nature in food production.
3. Eliminating food waste.

WWF didn't ask Tesco to fund a few environmental programs; they co-created solutions with the UK's food value chain, leveraging the strengths of both organisations to make an impact that neither could achieve alone. The clarity of the overarching vision has enabled the partnership to grow in new and innovative ways. For example, Tesco is now funding innovation grants to tech start-ups that can help reduce the environmental impact for the farmers in their supply chain. All dedicated to achieving that overarching vision.

Similarly, in the UK, a partnership between Boots, the high street chemist and Macmillan Cancer Support has a vision to ensure that support for those affected by cancer is only moments away.[3] Macmillan is leveraging the physical presence of Boots in every main street in the UK and their position as a source of trusted advice to provide direct support and access. The partnership includes training pharmacists to advise on the impacts of a cancer diagnosis and equipping beauty advisers to help cancer patients with the physical effects of treatment.

Creating a joint partnership vision is an invitation to collaborate deeply with your partner, rather than a solicitation for financial support. If you can grow your partnership from transactional program support to activities across all five pillars, you'll have a sustainable and transformational partnership that leverages all the skills, assets, resources and networks of your partner. It won't happen overnight, but you'll need to elevate your thinking to be more ambitious if you want to inspire greater commitment from your partner. Focusing on WHY you partner and the impact you could create together will take you further than the WHAT. Otherwise, you'll have a bunch of disjointed activities that don't yield the same impact for you, your cause and your beneficiaries.

Making a graceful exit

Linda is an incurable optimist. That's probably why she once tried a basketball bootcamp, despite being only five feet tall. The Dakota First Nations people have a saying, '*When you discover you are riding a dead horse, it's best to dismount*'. She really should have ditched bootcamp, but she stuck with it far too long, hoping to make it work.

When partnership managers are under pressure to meet tough targets, they can fall into the trap of riding multiple dead-horse partners and prospects in the hope they revive.

How do you know it's a dead horse and not just resting? Can you avoid the trap and dismount early?

Don't buy a stronger whip

Putting in greater time, effort and resources won't change the result if your partner is moribund. You can tell it's time to dismount when they don't engage with your events and invitations. Or they have relegated the relationship to a very junior person in the corporate team who doesn't have authority, budget or influence. Your emails and calls may go unanswered, and the corporate partner stubbornly resists your efforts to renew or grow their commitment.

The best decision is to look hard at the ROI of the partnership and conduct a clear-eyed review as to whether it still meets your needs. It may have been a great fit at the start, but things change over time. Choose to harvest or exit if the value is no longer there for you.

Don't try to change riders

It's easy to blame the partnership manager, but it's rarely the case that a change in jockey will reboot a failing relationship. If you have a competent team, the issue is more likely to be with the corporate partner and the value they perceive from the partnership. It may no longer fit their commercial needs, brand positioning or urgent priorities. Conduct an honest discovery meeting with your corporate partner to uncover if they're just going through a bad patch or if it's better to retire from the race.

Don't reset the performance standard

The mantra we often hear from partnership managers is that a 'partnership is all about awareness'. We usually find that a partnership is all about awareness after the corporate decides not to give you any cash.

Brand awareness is a useful benefit from a corporate partnership but should only be one pillar of value. If you try to reset the performance standards for the partnership, you're selling yourself and your organisation short. It's like running a dead horse because you've decided that you don't want to win the race. Set clear expectations for the partnership and make sure you check regularly that you're both on track.

Don't add more dead horses to increase the average speed

If you have a partnership portfolio of lifeless nags, adding more to the pile won't help you reach that stretch target. You'll end up wasting a lot of time and energy trying to resuscitate them at the expense of new opportunities that could be more valuable. It's a natural human instinct to avoid loss and preserve what you already have rather than take a risk on something unknown. But in this case, it will be a slow spiral of decline and you'll miss out on big, juicy new partnership prospects that deserve your time and focus.

Set aside time every year to take a hard look at the partnerships that no longer serve you. Make the decision now to thank your non-performing partners for their previous support and make a dignified exit. Better to dismount than flog a dead horse for the next financial year.

> **Better to dismount than flog a dead horse.**

How you exit will leave the door open for future opportunities if things change and make it more likely that a partner will recommend you to others. Celebrate what the partnership has achieved for each organisation and for the cause. Leave your partner feeling valued, recognised and honoured for their contribution. Even if the organisational partnership ceases, you may find that the corporate's employees will continue to support you individually into the future. Developing a good reputation for professional, well-managed partnerships will be a valuable asset for your non-profit's brand.

A well-nurtured relationship built on mutual understanding and respect will last over time. You can grow exceptional partnerships from a small base if the fundamentals are there and you have a clear view of future success. Not every partnership will be an award winner, but regular attention to nurturing and growing the relationship will ensure you get the maximum value for your effort, your cause and your partner.

CASE STUDY
Save the Children and GlaxoSmithKline

GlaxoSmithKline (GSK) is a global pharmaceuticals and health company with a mission to 'help people do more, feel better and live longer'. Save the Children (SCUK) is an international humanitarian aid and development agency focused on children. With a 98% brand recognition, it is one of the UK's best known and trusted charities.

The relationship between SCUK and GSK was solid, but firmly anchored in corporate philanthropy. GSK gave 20% of its profits in developing countries to promote better healthcare in each local market of operation and supported some SCUK projects in Kenya and the Democratic Republic of Congo (DRC). What did it take to shift from localised corporate philanthropy to a global, integrated partnership?[4]

In 2011, when the CEO of Save the Children spoke at the GSK annual leadership conference, he asked this bold question: 'We are the generation that can stop children dying of preventable diseases. Will you take on the challenge?' The CEO of GSK rose to accept the challenge and quickly convened a steering group of the most senior executives at each organisation to guide the partnership.

The focus areas were coalesced into a document with Five Pillars, each with its own working group of joint SCUK and GSK staff and with regularly scheduled meetings in each work stream. The early commitment of resources and support from the CEO and senior leadership were crucial in ensuring that the right people were available for the working groups.

The Five Pillars were:

1. Investment in programs
2. Core business and product development
3. Joint advocacy activities
4. Brand and commercial initiatives

Global employee engagement.

An ambitious goal was set for the partnership: *to help save one million children's lives.* This goal was further refined into four key objectives:

1. Widen immunisation reach for the hardest to reach communities
2. Increase in investment in training, reach and scope of health workers in the poorest countries
3. Address the nutrition needs of children in the poorest countries to prevent malnutrition
4. Develop an innovative partnership model to demonstrate best practice in the sector.

The goal and objectives reflected the synergies in the core business, mission and talents of each organisation. In addition, it tapped into the underlying aspiration of GSK to be the market leader in its field and to inspire a different way of thinking. An innovative partnership would reposition the GSK brand at the forefront of global health and enable SCUK to change the lives of many more children than it could reach alone.

Advocacy activities around global health are now conducted jointly by SCUK and GSK across the world. The activities focus on improving health systems and have been augmented by using GSK's assets in the DRC and Kenya and also in developed counties such as the UK and the USA.

Employee engagement in both organisations is high. There is a waiting list at SCUK to join the team managing the partnership. GSK employees have embedded staff fundraising as part of their core activities (the Pulse Program) and have raised over GB£5 million across 70 countries in the last ten years. SCUK can tap into the broad range of talents in GSK for skilled volunteering. This is not the tokenistic one or two days per year that many companies offer, but secondments of 6-12 months to solve important issues. Every GSK staff member becomes a partnership champion after the secondment and inspires further staff commitment among their colleagues.

The financial value of the partnership to SCUK has increased significantly. The original philanthropic partnership yielded approximately GB£200,000. By the end of 2015, the financial contribution had increased to over GB£7 million per annum. This did not include any of the new health products that were still in the pipeline or awaiting approval nor the value of services in kind. GSK is spending GB£16 million (approx. AU$31 million) to train 5000 health workers in remote Kenya and the DRC to improve childbirth practices and health services. The overall value of the partnership is now estimated at over GB£70 million.

GSK has used the partnership to relaunch its global brand and reinforce its core messages to its global market. It clearly considers that the partnership has added to its future market value and positioned it as a market leader in healthcare.

Most importantly, on its tenth anniversary in 2023, the partnership had reached 3.5 million children under five with live-saving health care.

The last word belongs to Dr Lisa Bonadonna, VP and head of the partnership at GSK. 'Nobody has ever said this challenge is too difficult. They just say, "We're going to do everything possible to make it happen".'

Conclusion

Corporate partnerships take time to develop and the full value of the relationship may not be seen in the first year. Thoughtful nurturing of the partnership and a willingness to adapt and grow with your partner will ensure a sustainable relationship and the maximum value for your effort.

Great partnerships can transform your cause and your impact, but things do change over time. Asking tough questions of each other can uncover any potential divergence in direction and aspirations, enabling you to create space for new opportunities. Being ambitious about the partnership vision and goals will challenge you and your partner and unlock innovation, new value and greater impact.

6

It Takes a Village

Tough Mudder is a light-hearted physical challenge involving kilometres of obstacles, fitness challenges and plenty of mud.[1] One of the main obstacles on the course is the wall. It's too high for even the biggest competitors to scale it. The solution lies in teamwork. One person needs to stand at the bottom so others can climb on their shoulders to reach the top. They then sit at the top and help to pull others up. At Tough Mudder, it's a given that complete strangers will help you over the wall; you don't need to rely on a friend or teammate. In this way, everyone succeeds, from the smallest to the strongest.

Corporate partnerships require a similar amount of combined effort but usually less mud. It takes a whole-of-organisation effort to identify, nurture, win and grow meaningful partnerships.

Partnerships present unique challenges

Non-profits embarking on corporate partnerships often fall into the trap of simply hiring a partnership executive, giving them a big income KPI and then waiting for the money to come in. That might work if you're selling cars or shoes, but it's not the right approach to partnerships.

A meaningful, big scale partnership will have multiple pillars of value that make it hard for a corporate to disengage. The corporate will be so entrenched in the partnership with your non-profit that they can't and won't simply trade you in for another partner every year. You build and create impact together as the relationship deepens. It means your partnership manager will deal with many different disciplines and departments in your corporate partner. They might include:

- Marketing and communications
- Sales team
- PR manager
- Media manager
- CSR/community team
- HR manager
- Product manager
- General manager or CEO.

Depending on the nature and aims of the partnership, it could be all of the above or some more intensively. Your corporate partner could ask your partnership manager to deliver a range of inputs and insights to fulfil the partnership requirements. A random sample might typically include:

- program reports
- impact reports
- event coordination
- field trip coordination
- communications and content
- media briefing
- joint PR release
- ambassador management
- expert speakers
- volunteer management
- data capture and financials
- campaign concept
- CEO/leadership liaison
- relationship plans.

For example, we worked on a cause marketing partnership with Procter & Gamble, in which a portion of the sales from each pack of Vicks products provided a donation to health and hygiene programs across the world. Bringing the partnership to life included a review of on-pack presentation and logos, in-store activation, staff volunteering, staff fundraising, a media event, digital promotions, printed collateral, presentations to staff and program visits. Collaboration and leveraging the expertise of our colleagues were critical to the partnership's success.

Partnerships represent unique challenges and opportunities. They don't behave like traditional fundraising, and they require a set of skills that can't possibly exist in one person, however talented. You need the whole organisation to be mobilised for corporate partnerships.

The main stumbling block is often a lack of knowledge. Your colleagues don't know that they are vital to the success of corporate partnerships. It's not in their job description or KPIs. They are experts in their fields and have no idea about how to work with corporates. In some cases, there is fear and trepidation about engaging with a corporate audience; in others, there is an ideological barrier where corporates are seen as the problem, not part of the solution. For partnership executives, it can sometimes feel like the internal relationships are more challenging than prospecting for new corporate partners.

There is an old story about British Prime Minister Winston Churchill leading a newly elected MP through the Houses of Parliament. When the MP pointed to the green benches in front, he asked, 'Is that where the enemy sits?' 'No, my boy,' replied Winston. 'That's where the opposition resides. The enemy sits behind us.'

It can be a lonely place for partnership executives without the support of their organisation. Their work is not understood and is not a priority for others to contribute. Partnership executives often try to fill the gaps themselves to ensure that the components of a partnership are delivered and the corporate relationship is preserved. That's a recipe for burnout, not a long-term strategy for partnership success. As one who once spent hours tying branded swing tags to gerberas for a 500-person partnership lunch, trust me, it's not sustainable.

The optimal approach is to seek help and mobilise the whole organisation for partnerships. That requires building understanding, alignment and commitment, and it starts from the top of your non-profit.

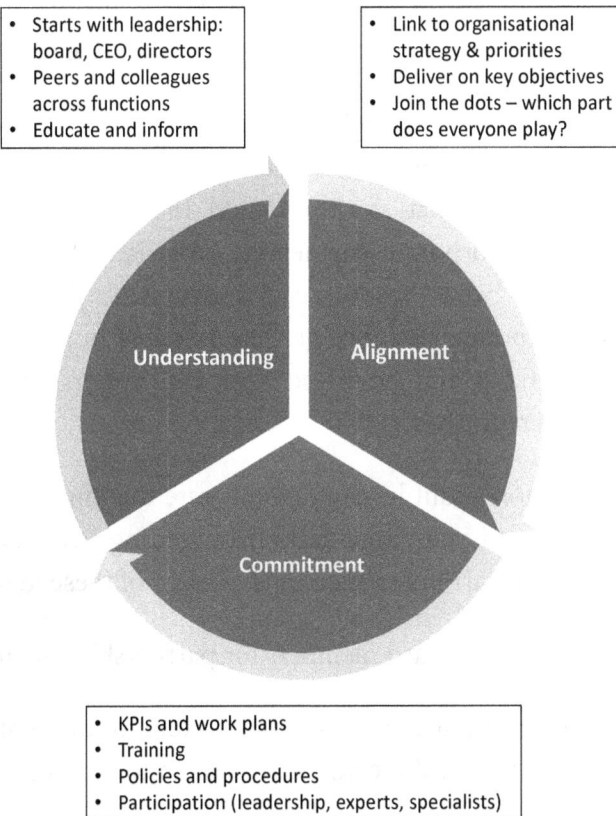

Figure 13: Optimal approach to partnerships

The role of leadership

The environment for successful partnerships starts with the CEO, leadership and board. They are busy people, juggling competing priorities and ensuring the organisation is financially viable. They are also unlikely to have any experience in corporate-community partnerships. Board members may come from corporate backgrounds, but it's a very different perspective when you don't have market power and must compete for attention. They don't realise it's difficult when you don't have a tangible product or service to sell.

They don't know enough and are generally time-poor. Partnership executives can help by regularly providing snippets of information. This could include case studies of successful corporate partnerships, the latest trends and highlights of what has succeeded and why. If you have existing corporate partners, get one to come in and talk to your leadership and board so they can understand your partner's perspective.

If you're a non-profit leader, demonstrate the importance of partnerships to your organisation by getting involved and removing the barriers to success. Try some of these ideas.

Provide access to board members for partnership executives.

Make corporate partnerships a regular item for discussion in leadership and board meetings. Add them to your agenda as a standing item.

Be available for meetings with corporate leaders and key decision-makers. A significant partnership will need peer-to-peer conversations at the very top.

Speak at key corporate events such as partnership launches and annual company conferences. As a non-profit leader, you are the principal storyteller for the organisation.

Leverage your own networks for introductions and connections and encourage board members to do the same.

Be realistic about the long lead time (usually 12-18 months) in building strategic corporate partnerships and develop KPIs accordingly.

Make sure you have a clearly articulated organisational strategy. A corporate partner won't come on the journey with you if you don't know where you're going or what's important.

Allocate appropriate resources to corporate partnership development. That includes competitive remuneration for partnership executives and a suitable budget for skills development, ongoing training and external support.

Build a culture of partnerships and relationship management at the heart of your organisation.

Don't be the leader who undermines the potential for corporate partnership with a lack of support or poor direction. Here are some things that partnership executives have said about their leaders:

'My boss has given me a list of the ASX Top 200 and told me to just cold call them.'

'A board member saw an article on a charity-corporate partnership in his in-flight magazine. Now he wants to know why we don't have one like it.'

'My CEO went on a business trip interstate and texted me pictures of corporate HQs and their logos. He thinks it's my new prospect list.'

'My manager sticks random ideas on my laptop with Post-it notes or leaves magazine articles with the same message. "Get us a partnership like this."'

'I feel like my CEO doesn't value the work I do. She's just after quick cash income and is putting pressure on me to hit some huge targets in the next three months.'

'Partnerships aren't a priority here and I can't get the help from other departments that I need.'

'I'm the sole fundraiser and I've got to do major gifts, regular giving and trust applications. Now, my boss has asked me to add corporate partnerships on my spare day.'

As a non-profit leader, you have multiple demands on your time. If you want the organisation to be successful in corporate partnerships, provide strategic direction, appropriate resources to partnership executives and a realistic expectation of the timeframe to build meaningful partnerships.

Recruit for success

Non-profit leaders adopt various approaches to recruitment when starting out in corporate partnerships. Some try to do it themselves as the organisational founder and general jack of all trades. Others hire someone as a general fundraiser and get them to stretch into corporate partnerships. They might find an agency that will go and hunt for corporate sponsors or take someone straight from a corporate role and give them partnerships. Or they might hire a dedicated partnership manager.

If you're the CEO and founder of a small organisation, you're used to doing everything yourself. How hard could it be to add corporate partnerships? Actually, if you don't have partnership skills or a previous corporate network, it could be time-consuming, frustrating and ultimately value-destroying.

Your time is better spent on getting crystal clear on your strategy and understanding what you need to achieve your big ambitions. When you understand what you need and where corporate partners fit, then you can decide whether the opportunity warrants the time and effort. But you'll quickly find that you need help.

Sponsorship agencies can offer to find corporates for you — for a fee or commission. Typically, they mine your database for contacts, tap a few likely suspects and leave you with some tactical partnerships that don't last.

Partnerships thrive on relationships, but who owns the relationship in this example? You've expanded the agency's contact list via access to your database and they've simply gathered the low-hanging fruit that you knew about already.

Be sceptical of anyone that promises instant results in corporate partnerships. Even if you gain a few new partnerships, you're the one who has to manage them into the future and it's your brand and reputation at risk.

Taking on someone who's a recent corporate refugee or a fundraiser used to traditional income raising will require an investment of time, support and training. They won't get it immediately and the learning curve can be steep. You'll need to allow a learning and development budget to build their skills and offer support to help them learn.

Professional, experienced partnership executives are worth the investment, but you'll need to offer them time and support to get to know your organisation. What worked in another non-profit may be very different for your organisation. Some bring the experience of nurturing partnerships in a bigger team with a more well-known brand. If you're a niche organisation with a small team, you'll have to manage their expectations of how self-reliant they'll need to be.

Recruitment for success in partnerships also extends to the board. Many non-profit boards are stuffed with sector experts, such as medical researchers, with a smattering of people with corporate skills in finance or legal. Marketing skills are scarce on the ground within most boards and experience in fundraising or partnerships is the mythical unicorn.

Boards need to be closely involved in significant corporate partnerships, so CEOs should consider this when recruiting to fill vacant board places. You don't necessarily need someone with an amazing corporate address book, but you do need people who are willing to show up to corporate events, support corporate prospecting at the right level and speak for the organisation with corporate partners.

If you're stuck with a board of specialist experts or, conversely, a range of corporate executives that see their role as purely governance (which is code for 'I don't want to do anything more than turn up to four meetings per year'), you may have to wait for vacancies to add the right mix of skills.

The other approach is to create a corporate advisory committee outside the board. In this way, you can invite people with genuine interest and corporate networks to offer their insights and expertise. Then give your partnership executive direct and regular access to them. Board renewal takes time, but you can shape the expectations for every newcomer and make sure that their KPIs include contributing to corporate partnerships.

Mobilise your colleagues

Corporate partnerships can take 12-18 months to nurture and bring to fruition. Even with a gold-standard set of connections and introductions, it will be at least six months. You have to adapt to the corporate's budget and decision cycles, and there's little you can do to hurry them up.

You might look really busy during that time, but your boss and colleagues won't see any results yet. Involving your colleagues early in the process helps to demystify corporate partnerships and allows them to offer their ideas and insights. Get them involved in brainstorming corporate prospects, tap into their information when you're building your asset catalogue or hold a network mapping session with a cross-section of colleagues to see who has warm connections to a prospect.

Internal stakeholder checklist

Stakeholder group	Support required	Actions
Board and executive	Introductions and referrals Speaking events Peer-to-peer relationship management Partnership launch or milestone celebration	Example: Brief the CEO Arrange intro meeting with corporate CEO

Stakeholder group	Support required	Actions
Marketing/ communications	Marketing collateral Communications content and channels Digital media content and execution Partnership campaign material PR and promotions Event management	Example: Prepare briefing for digital content Share timeline for launch
Call centre or switchboard	Manage inbound calls about a partnership/ campaign Modify call waiting messages for a campaign Answer partnership FAQs Direct or answer enquiries on workplace giving	Example: Give FAQs on the partnership to the call centre team
Finance	Timely financial reports on a partnership Acquittals, invoices and tax receipts	Example: Let the finance team know about the reporting requirements

Stakeholder group	Support required	Actions
HR and volunteers	Volunteer coordination Risk management procedures e.g. Working with Children check, OH&S Appropriate KPIs for staff involved in partnerships	Example: Brief the volunteer team on how many staff will be attending
Programs/ services	Program reports Content and storytelling Impact measurement Photos, stories and videos of programs or beneficiaries Subject matter expertise Keynote speakers at events Attend partner meetings	Example: Ask the programs/ services team to schedule content collection
Ambassadors or advocates	Speaking events Share digital partnerships news or content through social media networks PR opportunities Introduction to corporate networks	Example: Brief the ambassador on key speaking points for the partnership event

Provide clarity on which corporates you're looking for and why

The best way to fend off those unsolicited 'helpful' suggestions and random ideas is to be clear on what you're actually looking for. It's much easier to say, 'Thanks for the suggestion, but here's the shortlist we've identified. Can you help with any connections?' than shoot them down in flames. That means doing your homework early: gathering your assets, refining your value proposition and building a prospect list that's the right fit for your organisation.

Keep communicating

Be brave and be transparent. Don't be afraid to tell everyone what's going on. If your top five prospects haven't yielded anything yet, tell everyone and then tell them the next five you're after and why.

Use internal newsletters, staff forums or news boards to share what's going on. An information vacuum quickly fills with rumours, assumptions or speculation, which are not helpful to you or the organisation. You develop a communications plan for your corporate partners, and you need to consider a separate one for your internal stakeholders.

Build corporate partnerships into organisational processes

Sometimes, it's the simple things that build trust. I once made the point of including a presentation on corporate partnerships in every monthly induction session for new staff. That gave me the opportunity to set the scene early and build relationships with key people. If you've been successful at getting leadership support, then they can build partnership participation into key roles, job descriptions and performance measures.

Convene a working group

Everyone likes to be part of a success story. Whilst your colleagues may have no background in corporate entities, they have valuable skills and insights to contribute. If you have a significant partner or prospect, invite your colleagues to be part of a working group to explore how to bring this partnership to life. It means you're not chasing them down for vital elements or asking for things they didn't expect to deliver. You're not just working collaboratively and effectively; you're building their partnership skills by stealth and turning them into organisational advocates.

Bring a friend

If you already have some friendly corporate partners, invite one of them to speak at a team event. They can talk about the value of the partnership to their organisation, outline the support they need and remind your colleagues of the amazing outcomes you're achieving together. This is particularly effective if you can bring a corporate partner to a board or leadership team meeting. It will inspire them to get more involved and help them reflect on why partnerships are important to your organisation.

The particular challenges of a federated organisation

We often talk about partnerships needing a whole-of-team effort. It takes an extra level of effort and coordination when you work in an organisation that's a federated model, with independent organisations or members in each state, under the same brand. Too often, we hear of competition between states or branches, which can be a major obstruction to bigger partnerships. Corporates don't see the internal structures; they just want to partner with an organisation that operates in a consistent and professional manner.

The months of COVID lockdown yielded some great iso-baking results. But have you ever tried to bake something with too many cooks in the kitchen? Especially if they've all got slightly different cakes in mind and their own preferences. One person's pavlova is somebody else's sponge cake. The result is poorer for everyone – especially if you're fighting over the same eggs.

This is a frequent problem with developing partnerships in organisations with federated models. Whilst state-based entities do maintain stronger connections to local communities, they can run into difficulty when trying to win and nurture national corporate partnerships. There is often duplication, with different states talking to the same corporate. Even worse, there's outright competition for the same partner.

Federated structures can inhibit the full potential of corporate partnerships. Corporates only see one brand name and cause, whether it's heart health, vision impairment or sick children. They aren't interested in your internal structures; they simply want to align with your cause. But state-based entities, even with an overarching national head office, can be driven by different things. Leadership, priorities, culture and systems can all be slightly different. The differences might seem small, but like building the Sydney Harbour Bridge, a small variation can mean you don't meet in the middle when you're finished.

> The solution is to put the partner relationship at the centre.

The solution is to put the partner relationship at the centre. Good salespeople often talk about a customer-centric approach, which is exactly what federated organisations need to do with partnerships.

Consistent, standardised processes and systems

It helps if every state organisation uses the same processes and methodology with corporate partners. There are too many examples where a national head office and a state organisation disagree on whether a corporate partner fits their risk profile and appetite. Similarly, take a consistent approach to nurturing and growing relationships.

The corporate partner isn't interested in your internal politics; it wants to be valued and managed in the same professional way across your organisation. Just because the opportunity didn't originate in your state doesn't mean you shouldn't commit resources to growing it. The outcome for your cause will be a far greater impact.

Centralised approach to relationship management

Someone must take the lead in managing the corporate partnership. It does require a team approach, but there needs to be one main cook in the kitchen somewhere. In managing global partnerships with Save the Children there was a 'home donor' rule. Wherever the corporate was headquartered and the main relationship initiated, that office took the lead in coordinating and managing the partnership. Every other national office contributed to the working group and supported the partnership in their location. There was appropriate revenue sharing depending on the rollout of the partnership, but the lead relationship team guided everyone.

Corporates like the opportunity to deal face-to-face with a key charity. It makes it easier to allow the state or location where the corporate is headquartered to take the lead with the relationship. You can invite them to events, facilitate site visits and nurture the relationship easier. That's why the Save the Children office in Sweden managed the IKEA global partnership and the team in the UK took the lead with Unilever.

If your corporate partner is headquartered in Sydney, let the NSW team lead the relationship. If it's in Perth and they only have a small team, let them lead but offer support from across the federation. Respect the local relationships that can be built through face-to-face interactions and help them be successful.

You can turn a geographically dispersed organisation to your advantage. Your local knowledge and community presence can offer a grassroots perspective and credibility in addition to a national footprint. For those corporate partners that always like to see money spent in their home state, you can offer authentic local solutions to augment the national approach.

Enabled and supported partnerships

Technology, customer relationship management (CRM) systems and culture enable a consistent and rewarding partner experience. If your organisation has mismatched systems and CRMs, work around it with shared tools like Basecamp or Squarespace. The most important element is a culture that enables collaboration and prioritises the partner experience. How can you ask a partner to collaborate if you're all fighting each other?

By placing the partner experience at the centre of the relationship, not making it work around your organisation's structure, you will get exponentially more value from the partnership. You'll get a bigger commitment of income and value, better profile for your brand and greater impact for your cause. If you force your partner to work around your internal barriers, they'll eventually decide it's all too hard and go somewhere else. Large corporates have enough of their own internal silos, they don't want to have to deal with yours too.

Overcoming organisational boundaries

It is perfectly possible to work together across boundaries to win a high-value, significant partnership. We did it years ago with Save the Children and we managed to coordinate internationally, across countries. Here are some insights gained along the way.

Leverage senior leadership support

All the senior leaders must be on board across your organisation because the corporate partner will need relationship contacts at every level. Leaders provide visible support through events, meetings with peer executives and public statements. They also need to shift priorities and allocate resources to make the partnership successful. Your corporate partner wants to see that the organisation is truly committed to the partnership and it can't be done solely from the partnership executive level.

Build a coalition

If you're going after a national partnership, you want everyone at the table — communicating often and sharing expertise and insights. You may have partnership managers in each state who manage local relationships but you'll need a collaborative approach to a large corporate with national reach. Regular forums and simple protocols can create trust between teams. You will have a primary relationship manager for the partnership, but everyone must be on the same page about their role to support it.

When we worked on the global partnership with Procter & Gamble (P&G), our working group decided that Australia and New Zealand would be the first countries to go live with a cause marketing campaign. We like to think they considered Australians as early adopters, but we suspect that the P&G HQ also thought that if it failed, then no one would notice! The campaign was a success, and we were able to feed insights and learnings back to the USA office so they could refine the bigger American rollout to come. The working group met regularly, shared information generously and supported each other. The total raised from the global campaign was in the millions at the end, which funded life-saving health programs across the world.

Agree revenue sharing and KPIs

This is always a sticky point in a federated or dispersed model. Each member organisation is independent, with its own revenue targets, reporting to a different board. But again, the corporate partner only sees the same name, same brand and logo everywhere, and expects you to behave nationally.

The Save the Children global partnership coalition developed revenue-sharing protocols across national boundaries. Revenue earned in each location was attributed to profit and loss there, but a percentage was returned to the home HQ country to cover the costs of the principal relationship management activities.

Some organisations have moved to a national model to remove some of the difficulties of a federated model. But if it can be done across national boundaries, with teams from Sweden, Italy, India, USA, UK, Australia and Japan, then there's no reason it can't be done across a single country. Corporates buy into your mission and want to do something significant for the community. Don't let your internal organisational structure stand in the way. Put some simple processes in place and you won't be relegated to local business relationships.

If you want meaningful corporate partnerships that sustain over the long term, take the approach of a fine dining restaurant. There are clear accountabilities, a system for communicating and working and a singular focus on the end customer. Otherwise, you'll present a dinner with overdone steak and undercooked vegetables, whilst dessert never makes it to the table.

The costs and benefits of mobilising your village

Even the biggest competitors can't make it over the Tough Mudder wall alone. It's not about size; it's about how well you can mobilise all your combined resources, skills, energy and focus to achieve something that seems impossible. If you hire a partnership executive and expect them to scale the wall by themselves, you'll see them try valiantly but slide back to the ground every time. You'll not only miss out on the transformational opportunities of partnerships, but it will have negative impacts on your organisation and your people, including:

- burnout and stress
- frequent turnover in staff and higher recruitment costs
- discontinuity in relationship management with corporate partners
- loss of relationship knowledge
- creating unnecessary break points in the relationships
- lower trust and understanding
- partnerships that don't grow
- income stuck or plateaued
- negative impacts on your brand as you're not seen as a reliable community partner.

If you work to get it right, the payoff will be enormous. By mobilising your village, you will build corporate partnerships into your organisational DNA. It will make your non-profit stand out from the crowd of needy non-profits and position you as a credible and trustworthy partner. You will attract more corporate partners as your reputation for partnerships grows. You will be able to ask for greater commitment from corporate partners and stretch their ambitions for new and innovative work. You'll attract the best talent, as people want to be part of a winning team. Most importantly, you'll achieve transformational outcomes for your beneficiaries, your cause and the world.

Conclusion

Partnerships require help from the whole organisation to be successful. Leaders play a critical role in creating a culture of partnerships, setting realistic expectations and providing the necessary supporting systems. Boards and executives have a big impact, even if they don't have a magic address book of corporate contacts. Beyond helping with introductions or nurturing relationships they need to set a clear organisational strategy and remove the barriers to success. With the right support and direction at the top, your non-profit is set for partnership success.

7

Hello from the Other Side

When Linda's children were small, a weekend stopover in Amsterdam broke the mind-numbing monotony of a long-haul flight to the UK in economy class. She excitedly showed them the canals, the architecture and the glorious Van Gogh Museum. When she asked her son what he liked best about the trip, what did he say? 'Mum, they served hot chips in a cone, with mayonnaise instead of tomato sauce!' She'd failed to appreciate the perspective of a seven-year-old. For him, the joys were in the small things.

The management writer Charles Handy once flippantly compared a British workgroup to a rowing team: eight people going backwards, without talking to each other, steered by someone at the front who wasn't doing much work. His perspective was challenged by an oarsman in the audience. 'It's quite the opposite,' asserted the rower, 'it's the perfect example of a good team. The rowers wouldn't have the confidence to try so hard if they didn't have absolute trust in each other and in the small person at the front who did the steering.'[1]

Perspective comes naturally to some, but others need a prompt to know what to look for and the types of questions to ask. Perspective is an important ingredient for successful partnerships. Building meaningful relationships that will sustain over time requires a deep understanding of your partner and a willingness to step into their shoes for a while.

Them and us. It's tempting to think of corporates as hard-nosed, impersonal profit-making machines. But those organisations are filled with living, breathing humans trying their best to get through the day. Non-profits don't have a monopoly on compassion, ingenuity or virtue. If you're building corporate partnerships, try to understand what's happening on their side of the fence.

Here's a light-hearted peek into the other side.

Dear Partnership Manager,

I'm the CSR and community engagement manager for ACME Retail. ACME is a $300 million listed company with multiple brands and outlets across Australia and the Pacific. I've got a team of three people, all part-time, who work with me.

Sorry that I haven't replied to your five emails and calls yet. My kids are at home sick and the dog just chewed through my modem cable. I've spent the last two days in a virtual 'strategy away day' that the HR team thought would be good for team building. Team drinks whilst dressed in a pirate costume were just what I needed as my kids tried to burn down the kitchen.

What was it you wanted? I got to the end of your email trail and still didn't know. Any chance you could be a bit more succinct? A couple of paragraphs would be great, as I've got another 400 emails in my inbox today. By the way, did you know that three other people in your charity also emailed me recently? Which one of you should I answer?

You might think we've got money to burn, but the vulture capital firm that bought out the company last year is squeezing us for more return. Every dollar spent has to be justified. There have been two rounds of redundancies and every team is having to do more with fewer staff. Morale is a bit low at the moment (see the HR initiative above). How can you help keep staff engaged and motivated to work with us?

I'm really interested in what you do. But it's not unique, trust me. I've had five approaches from similar organisations in the last fortnight. Can't you guys just work together? No, a table at your gala ball is not a unique opportunity. Champagne, a hotel room and Chris Hemsworth is a unique opportunity.

I'd love to promote your latest campaign/event/fundraiser in my internal comms. But I have to fight for space with every other department, including the compliance department with their latest compulsory training, the CEO's weekly update and HR's reiki healing wellness initiative. I need at least two months of lead time and some great content from you to cut through.

Community giving is only one part of my focus. I'm also working on modern slavery in the supply chain, measuring our response to the SDGs and creating a sustainability plan. Where do you fit in our strategy? Tell me how you can help.

Yes, it would be great to do online round-up donations for your charity and promote you on our website. But behind the scenes, our website is a bit of a sh*tshow. The digital team outsourced it to this hipster agency in Newtown and every time we make changes, it costs us a fortune. I need a really good business case to justify the effort.

I know we've got a lot of customer traffic in our stores and I'm sure they'd love to buy your merchandise. But Gerald, the sales manager, has final say on what goes in stores and he's maximising every inch of space. Show me how your campaign is going to add to foot traffic and I'll be able to twist his arm. If you want us to create bespoke merchandise, then we'll need a 12-month lead time, as everything is manufactured in Bangladesh. Yes, I know it's only July, but the Christmas range is already locked down. Get in quick for summer 2025.

Personally, I think climate change, hunger, homelessness, cancer and kids' education are all really important and I do want to help. I'm inspired by the work you do - it must be great working in your charity. Help me to help you. Show me why you're a good fit for my organisation and help me demonstrate to my CEO the value you bring and the impact we could make together. I need to provide regular reports on any partnership, so make sure you've got some outcomes I can measure and describe.

I'd like to build a relationship with you. I need to know I can count on you to deliver what you say you can. Get to know me and maybe we can both achieve what we want.

Got to run. I've got my 10th Zoom meeting for the day and the CEO needs a briefing for the board. Maybe I shouldn't have signed up for Dry July and Weight Watchers this year.

Sincerely,

Jay Goodfellow

Your future corporate partner

Understanding your corporate audience

Corporate partnerships are not like philanthropy. You're not trying to connect with personal preferences on a cause that impacts someone emotionally. Partnerships are a mix of heart and science, but most importantly, you need to offer value in return. To create that value and make it commercially compelling for a corporate, you need to understand their motivations, priorities and needs. You don't need prior corporate work experience, although it can help. Instead, be willing to ask the right questions, learn and collaborate. If you can develop a deep understanding of the corporate perspective and how it changes over time, you're a long way towards building some very significant partnerships.

What's keeping corporate CEOs awake at night?

Corporate leaders don't usually elicit much sympathy. They are seen as a privileged, powerful elite cocooned from the day-to-day problems of ordinary mortals. However, the business landscape has changed rapidly and dramatically and many corporate leaders are struggling to keep up.

There is a plethora of issues for them to worry about beyond just keeping operations going and the company profitable. Here is a summary of the biggest issues facing business today:

Figure 14: The biggest issues facing business

Operations

The economic environment is turbulent and extraordinary forces, such as the Ukraine conflict and natural disasters, have severely impacted supply chains. The model of global connectivity for businesses is being challenged and input costs are soaring.

At the same time, governments are imposing more stringent standards for operations and corporates need to raise their standards of compliance. These include obligations under the Modern Slavery Act, gender equality and environmental standards. Investor focus on ESG requires big companies to improve their practices and reporting or risk disinvestment. Mid-sized companies are trying to keep up and remain competitive. Compliance adds to costs, time and resource allocations. The longer-term outcomes for society are positive, but there are near-term challenges for corporates along the way.

Marketing

It's hard to reach consumers, especially Millennials and GenZ. Where previous generations reliably read newspapers and watched TV, the latest generations inhabit multiple platforms — often at the same time. It's very expensive for corporates to reach this elusive audience. Once they do, engagement needs to be authentic and values-driven, or corporates risk their instant wrath on social media. Cancel culture strikes fear into the hearts of many corporate CEOs. At the start of the Ukraine war, over a thousand corporates exited or scaled back their operations in Russia.[2] Those that did not, or were too slow in the eyes of consumers, faced boycotts and a hail of negative press. Audiences are hard to reach, hard to please and cost much more to acquire.

People

There is a war for talent across many industries. The costs of retention are rising and it takes more than free beer and a ping-pong table to keep employees engaged. COVID caused everyone to reassess their priorities and many changed jobs, careers and locations. Employees are demanding better conditions, including flexibility and work-from-home options. An anxious and restive workforce is not a recipe for business success.

By 2025, Millennials will make up 75% of the workforce.[3] This generation wants to know whether an employer aligns with their personal values and expects the organisation to walk the talk. Meaningful commitments to environment and sustainability, diversity and inclusion and a strong employee value proposition are key to attracting and retaining talent.

Staff engagement has emerged as one of the biggest challenges facing corporates in a post-COVID world. The consequences of staff shortages, turnover and poor employer reputation will be very costly indeed.

The payoff for getting it right

Working in partnerships with non-profits can authentically demonstrate a corporate's social purpose. It can also unlock higher performance across multiple business areas, improve the employee value proposition, increase talent attraction and retention, and decrease staff turnover costs. More talented people means greater innovation and competitive advantage.

The best partnerships also improve operational efficiency, reduce waste and limit the harm to the community and the environment of production practices. Partnerships that bring new audiences or deepen engagement with core stakeholders will attract new customers and investors and increase corporate profits. The benefits to a corporate are multifaceted;

it's time for non-profits to start leading with those benefits, not their funding needs.

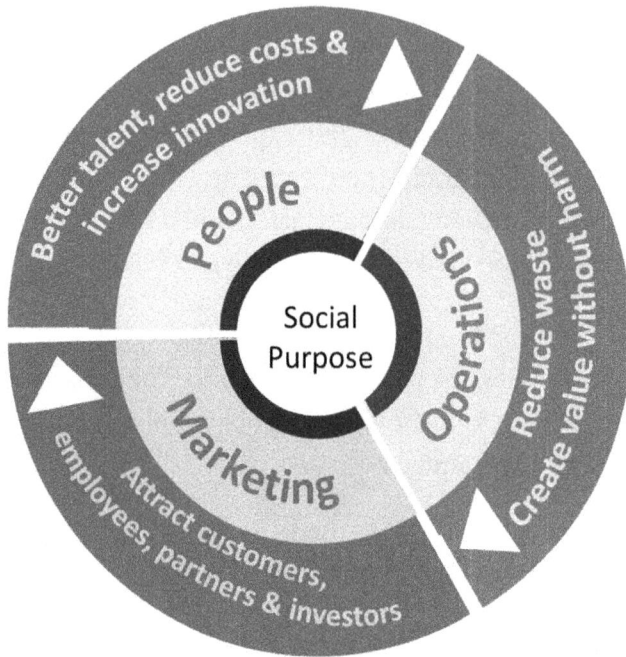

Figure 15: The partnership payoff

You have more in common than you realise

Our country friend Kate says her favourite maxim is, 'Don't look over the fence into the next paddock'. It's her way of saying that the grass might look greener, but you'll spend too much time obsessing about the neighbour's paddock to look after your own properly. But what if you peer over the fence and you find that your neighbour is having the same problems? Would it help you to develop empathy for their situation and even want to lend a hand?

A recent report shows the following situation for a group of people working in social impact:

- 61% are working longer hours
- 50% have experienced burnout
- 46% fear not meeting expectations
- 17-19% report low morale, mental health concerns and employee turnover.

Does this sound familiar? Could this be your non-profit? Is this you?

Actually, these people are corporate social responsibility professionals working in corporates.

The results come from the latest CSR insights survey from the US Association of Corporate Citizenship Professionals.[4] The report shows continual instability and change, increased demands and responsibilities and insufficient headcount. Over 60% of CSR professionals work in teams of five or fewer. They report needing more people, financial resources and greater buy-in from leadership.

It sounds like every non-profit I've ever worked with.

> An approach led by empathy and understanding will get a warmer reception.

There is a myth that CSR professionals are sitting on limitless buckets of money and are dying to get your unsolicited proposal. If you want to connect with CSR people to explore a corporate partnership, an approach led by empathy and understanding will get a warmer reception.

Here are three ways to make a meaningful connection.

Give them a compelling business case

CSR teams don't have big budgets and usually have to take budget approvals far up the line. Often, the final sign-off comes from their CFO, CEO, or someone far removed from the day-to-day understanding of social impact. You need to help them with a clear and compelling commercial proposition. They may love your organisation, be passionate about your cause and be willing to be a volunteer. However, they must convince internal stakeholders that your partnership proposal will be worth the investment. Show that you've understood the business needs and priorities and how the partnership will be a win-win. Do the work for your CSR contact and they'll be a more effective advocate.

Give them great content

Partnerships are a mix of head and heart. If the CSR team has managed to get sign-off on your partnership, they'll need your support to keep their executive, colleagues and customers inspired. Great quality content, in the form of images, video, stories and testimonials, is vital. CSR teams can build a strong pipeline for their marketing and communications department, which will convert your content to regular pieces across all corporate channels. Don't make them beg for content. Make it easy, regular and inspiring. You'll help the CSR team convert the marketing department to advocates and you'll increase brand awareness for your cause.

Understand their limitations

A bit of empathy will go a long way. If CSR professionals are experiencing many of the same challenges as you, then be considerate about how you work with them. In one survey, 86% of respondents said they have taken on more responsibilities during the past year without additional resources.[5]

Make sure you know how they like to be contacted so you don't pepper them with emails. Ask your CSR contact what they need to be successful with their leadership. Give them a generous shout-out on social media channels and thank them for their support. Invite them to a special event. Remember that they're hard-working humans like you, trying their best in challenging circumstances. They are allies, not gatekeepers.

The grass isn't always greener in the next paddock. If you understand that partnership teams and CSR people often face similar challenges, you'll be able to reach out with empathy. That's a great place to start in building a relationship.

Solve, don't sell

Competition among non-profits for corporate partnerships will likely intensify in the post-COVID-19 economy. However, there will be plenty of exciting opportunities for those with the right approach: that means a shift from 'selling' your programs or services to uncovering the problems that the corporate is encountering and how you can collaborate to solve them together. Economic turbulence means less budget available for corporate philanthropy but an appetite for real strategic alignment.

Consider the challenges outlined previously. How can a partnership with your non-profit help to mitigate the impact or become part of the solution? For example, a grassroots theatre in Sydney worked with a large bank to offer volunteering opportunities for their local staff. It inspired the staff to get more involved in the local community, provided a catalyst for people working remotely to come together and encouraged staff to re-engage with each other and the office environment.

Consider how your non-profit's expertise, assets, locations and networks can provide ways to address a corporate's high-priority business issues. You will shift the discussion from small philanthropic CSR budgets to bigger commitments embedded in the core business. And you won't need to do the hard sell on a partnership.

Common themes and trends in partnerships

Some themes and trends emerging from recent discussions with corporate clients are surprisingly consistent.

Fewer, more strategic partnerships

Most corporates don't have the time to deal with a filing cabinet full of relationships. They are refining their relationships and choosing a smaller list of partners that are truly aligned with their business. It enables them to develop deeper relationships, more meaningful impact and increased internal and external coherence. It makes it easier for staff, customers and investors to see the logic of their investment and demonstrate the corporate's authentic commitment to the chosen causes.

Corporate budgets are lean

Most businesses try to run as efficiently as possible. There are rigorous processes for reviewing and approving expenditure and investors will scrutinise whether it provides meaningful return.

The chief sustainability and corporate affairs officer of one large corporate told us: 'I've had many a conversation with people outside of Bupa who thought we're sitting on a goldmine of a couple of millions of dollars that we can just give out because we made a profit last year. It doesn't work like that. It really doesn't. I don't have a secret bank full of gold coins to dish out.'

Do your research

Workplaces are busy. Research shows that a typical worker will be distracted every three minutes and will probably never have a full hour to themselves without being interrupted.[6] Don't waste their time with unnecessary questions about things that are already in their annual report. Do your research and find out their financial reporting cycles. Many corporates publicly state on their websites the priority areas they are interested in. Do some basic due diligence and make sure your partnership approach is professional, relevant and shows appropriate respect for their time.

Get to know us

Pick your moments; understand the timeframes for proposals and the budget cycle. Wherever possible, conduct discovery meetings and be open to learning about the corporate's needs, priorities and planning schedules.

The senior director of sustainability and social impact at CSL says, 'Don't just send us a proposal without speaking to us. Get to know us a little bit more and find out where we're heading, who we are and what our focus areas are. Most of the information is online, yet it's quite amazing how many requests we get that just don't align with who we are as an organisation.'

Plan for the longer term

Budgets are set for multiple years ahead, so don't expect a corporate to fit you in immediately. Your urgent funding gap is not their priority. For example, Bupa and CSL's planning processes can lock in partnerships and activities for the next three years. If you'd like to be a strategic partner, start early and be prepared to nurture the relationship for longer than your own budget cycles. Think and plan for both the medium and longer term.

Demonstrate meaningful impact

Shift your non-profit from measuring activities to measuring impact. Corporates have to show stakeholders that the investment has been worth it. They also need clear impact metrics to meet their ESG reporting requirements. If the corporate is investing in your non-profit over multiple years, there must be meaningful impact and improvement to show how the partnership is making a difference.

Invest in the relationship

Justin is the sustainability manager at Cobram Estate Olives. He commented that 'Securing a partnership is only half the battle; maintaining and growing it is equally important.

Transparency upfront can be beneficial. Sharing your cards early on helps prevent partnerships from unravelling later when interests diverge.'

Things can change rapidly and key contacts move on. Invest in nurturing the relationship with regular contacts, reviews and opportunities to collaborate. The hard work starts after the contract is signed.

The best questions to ask each other

US President Thomas Jefferson had it right when he said, 'Truth between candid minds can never do harm'.

As you develop relationships with your partners, move beyond the basics that established the partnership. If you want a relationship that lasts decades, you cannot ask the same things year after year. If you're just just after more money each time, your partner will dread your call.

Here are the best questions to advance and deepen your partnership.

Is it having the impact we want?

Things change over time and there will be bumps along the way. Checking in with your partner and being candid about your joint achievements will create trust, transparency and greater commitment to the best outcomes for you and the community.

What benefits are you getting from the partnership?

When you negotiated the partnership, you probably included a bunch of benefits like PR, content, expertise or access to key audiences. You won't have visibility of the full range of benefits that a corporate is getting and there may be some unintended ones. Cancer Council Victoria worked with Commonwealth Bank (CBA) staff to change how they supported people experiencing financial hardship as a result of their diagnosis. It not only benefitted CBA customers but had the effect of improving the way that the bank dealt with a range of customers with similar issues. It improved CBA's customer retention and net promoter score and their staff satisfaction soared. The partnership allowed staff to feel proud and inspired about doing something meaningful to improve people's lives.

What's the most important thing to you?

Our world is volatile and complex and things are changing fast. Corporate leaders move on, companies merge or restructure and markets evolve. A corporate's priorities may well have changed and they need to refocus. Keep checking in to ensure you're still delivering to their needs and your own.

Are we being ambitious enough?

Early wins in the partnership are great and you can celebrate together. How can you challenge and stretch each other if you want the partnership to grow? Community needs aren't getting smaller, so how can the partnership respond?

How can we use our collective assets better?

As you get to know each other, you'll uncover new ways to leverage your expertise, networks and assets. Beyond Blue and Australia Post have a well-established partnership. During the Sydney Pride celebrations, Beyond Blue invited Australia Post to share their prized mardi gras float.[7] It was an opportunity that Australia Post wouldn't have been able to access by themselves, enabling employees to participate and the organisation to celebrate its LGBTIQ+ community.

How are your staff/customers/stakeholders feeling about the partnership?

You and your main contacts may think the partnership is going swimmingly, but what about the corporate's external stakeholders? Or your own non-profit donors? Find ways to get their feedback and input, and you'll uncover ways to tweak and improve your communications and partnership impact.

How can we make the impact sustainable?

No corporate wants to feel like an important program or initiative will fall over the moment they leave. They want to create a legacy that endures. That may involve bringing other stakeholders into the relationship, for example, universities, government and researchers. With ESG metrics a hot topic for corporate leaders, the ability to measure and plan for long-term success is critical to sustaining a longer-term relationship.

It's easy to get comfortable in a long-term relationship. But without the right questions, you could find that you've drifted apart over time. Note the shift from first-person, 'I' statements that often dominate early conversations, 'I think', 'I want', 'I need', 'I can offer...'.

Now, the emphasis is on 'We' as the partnership becomes an invitation to collaborate, not a bilateral exchange of value. If you create a space for collaboration and co-creation, you're on the right path to celebrating a long and fruitful relationship.

Conclusion

You don't need experience working in corporates to understand their world. Indeed, for many non-profits, it can seem like an alien universe and a foreign language. But partnership success depends on your willingness to see their perspective, acknowledge their priorities and develop empathy for a corporate's challenges.

When a corporate sees you as an ally, they will be open to the possibilities of what you can achieve for each other and the community. They will view you as part of the solution, not just selling something that is discretionary spend at best. It's not about your non-profit; it's about them. The better you get to know them, the more successful you'll be in winning partnerships.

Afterword

Non-profit organisations are working diligently on some of the biggest and thorniest issues facing our world, but they are not miracle makers. Challenges such as poverty, inequity, hunger or climate change will only be solved through collaboration with the communities impacted and those with the biggest resources and influence. In the 21st century, corporates — not governments — have the competency, trust and resources to create the change we need.

Corporate partnerships offer so much more than new funding. They can be transformational for your organisation and your cause. For too long, they have been the wallflowers on the dance floor whilst the cool kids in fundraising hogged the spotlight. Corporate partnerships are a unique combination of head and heart and don't behave like traditional fundraising. It's time to recognise the special qualities of corporate partnerships and develop an approach that unlocks the range of value and impact they offer.

Some non-profits have dabbled in corporate philanthropy or sponsorship with varying results. Many organisations apply the same approach as for high net worth donors, focusing on emotional cases for support. Other non-profits have never started in partnerships, viewing them as too hard or too complex. Realising the full potential of corporate partnerships requires a strategic approach and a shift in thinking from your own organisational needs to a commercial proposition that creates value for the corporate partner and a shared social impact.

The landscape for corporate partnerships is changing rapidly and non-profits must adapt and elevate their approach to be successful. The size of the prize is significant, with corporate giving in Australia alone estimated at over AU$5 billion per annum.

If you'd like a share of this prize and want to leverage the cash, networks, assets, audiences and resources of the corporate sector for your cause, there's no better time to get started.

We've discussed a simple three-step process to building successful corporate partnerships: Find, Win and Grow.

FIND is the first step to building the foundations for corporate partnerships. Internal reflection on your organisation's strengths, needs, assets and offerings is critical to aligning partnerships with your goals, priorities and aspirations. This internal work is often the difference between success and failure in corporate partnerships. It enables your non-profit to present a credible and compelling commercial value proposition to corporate partners instead of a tactical appeal for cash. A thoughtful and proactive approach to risk management helps protect your non-profit from the risks of poorly aligned partners that negatively impact your reputation. You will be able to focus on the corporates that best fit your organisational values, goals and risk appetite, and use your limited time and resources for maximum return.

WIN is a methodology for researching, connecting and securing new corporate partners. It encourages non-profits to abandon the traditional fundraising ask. Instead, you are guided through a process of discovery and collaboration that uncovers corporate needs, priorities and pain points. Your non-profit will be positioned as the solution to corporate problems rather than an inconvenient discretionary budget item. This approach unlocks greater value for your non-profit beyond program support and sets up the partnership for future growth.

GROW outlines the importance of nurturing corporate relationships and provides practical tools and approaches to maximising value for both partners. It enables your non-profit to inspire your corporate partners, create an ambitious vision for the partnership and build a sustainable relationship for the long term. Importantly, you'll have the methodology to reposition underperforming partners and make the tough decisions about where to spend your time and effort.

Two key elements underpin the Find, Win, Grow approach to strategic partnerships.

The first is the importance of mobilising your whole organisation to support partnerships. Partnership executives often find it easier to make hundreds of cold approaches to corporates than manage internal stakeholders. Partnerships are an ensemble performance, not a solo act. The range of stakeholders involved from the corporate side means that it's impossible for one person to manage. Partnerships are a whole-of-team effort to build multi-layered relationships that last over time.

Non-profit leadership plays an important role in success. Whilst it's useful if leaders and boards have corporate connections, it's more important for them to make the right decisions about budgets, performance targets, resourcing and support for partnerships. Effective leadership support is critical for any partnership program and will prevent the cycle of frustration and burnout that emerges when partnership executives are not appropriately supported.

The second key element is an understanding of the corporate perspective. The environment in which corporates operate is turbulent and challenging, particularly post pandemic. Corporate leaders are under pressure from their staff, customers and investors to demonstrate their contribution to the community.

The emergence of ESG, changes in government legislation, the war for talent and the rising expectations of consumers combine to make it hard for corporates to do business in the same way. They can't do it alone and need your non-profit to help. Non-profits who gain insights into the core priorities, challenges and ambitions of corporate partners will be well positioned for deeper and more collaborative partnerships.

The world urgently needs more collaboration and a willingness to work with groups that are unfamiliar or uncomfortable. If non-profits want to deliver on the miracles that the community demands, they need to work with the corporate sector. The much-needed breakthrough will be a strategic, thoughtful approach to corporate partnerships that is open to co-creating solutions.

Partnerships are being reimagined for the 21st century. There's no better time to get started.

Work with us

Stellar Partnerships specialises in sustainable and profitable partnerships between corporates and non-profits. We build partnerships for good, that deliver real business results and lasting social impact.

We provide coaching, skills training, partnership facilitation, strategy development and keynote speaking for conferences. Some of the things we can help with include:

- Getting started in partnerships for the first time
- Revitalising a partnership program that's got stuck
- Sharpening your team's partnership skills or coaching for your partnership challenges
- Growing your existing partnerships from good to great

- Educating and influencing board and leadership
- Facilitating workshops with your key partners to uncover more value
- Inspiring and motivating audiences about partnership possibilities.

Contact us at www.stellarpartnerships.com or connect with us linkedin.com/stellarpartnerships

About the Authors

Linda Garnett

Linda is an author, facilitator, strategist and thinker. She spent over two decades in corporate strategy and investment banking, working with big deals and even bigger egos. Her clients included central banks, international agencies, governments and global corporates. After learning what makes businesses tick and where the money is buried, she looked for ways to change the world rather than buy it.

Linda took her skills to the non-profit sector to help organisations be more commercial in their approach. She co-founded Stellar Partnerships to bridge the gulf in understanding between corporates and non-profits; two tribes who rarely speak each other's language.

Linda is obsessed with the potential of corporate-community partnerships to transform a cause, create real social impact and maximise commercial value. She believes collaboration is the only way to solve the big issues facing our world.

In her spare time, Linda loves travel and new experiences. She has travelled to 40 countries and can order food and beer fluently in each. Once she is done with flying planes, tap dancing, and embarrassing her children, she plans to spend her twilight years launching a leadership coup in the nursing home.

Get in touch with Linda at:

linda@stellarpartnerships.com

linkedin.com/in/lindagarnett2

Sharon Dann

Sharon has been a career fundraiser working with non-profits for over twenty years. She loves partnerships because they challenge her creative brain. They're part fundraising, part marketing, part sales and a whole lot of fun when you start to see the difference they make to your non-profit and your beneficiaries.

Sharon has worked on partnerships in the UK and Australia and raised millions of dollars for different organisations.

Since co-founding Stellar Partnerships, Sharon has worked with huge, well-established charities such as Beyond Blue, The Salvation Army and Legacy and small, volunteer-led charities such as Pet Medical Crisis. She loves to see people put the Stellar system into action and get awesome results.

Outside of work, Sharon is a proud solo mum to a gorgeous seven-year-old. Sharon loves running, cooking and painting, although not all at the same time.

Get in touch with Sharon at:

sharon@stellarpartnerships.com

linkedin.com/in/sharondann

References

INTRODUCTION

1. Helder, C. (2020). *Useful belief : because it's better than positive thinking.* Milton: John Wiley & Sons Australia, Ltd.

CHAPTER 1

1. Friedman, M. (1970). 'A Friedman Doctrine: The Social Responsibility of Business is to Increase Its Profits', *The New York Times Magazine*, viewed October 2023, https://www.nytimes.com/1970/09/13/archives/a-friedman-doctrine-the-social-responsibility-of-business-is-to.html

2. McLeod, J. (2018). *The Support Report,* JBWere.

3. Victor, D. (2017). 'Pepsi Pulls Ad Accused of Trivializing Black Lives Matter', *The New York Times,* viewed October 2023, https://www.nytimes.com/2017/04/05/business/kendall-jenner-pepsi-ad.html

4. Miller, K & Li, E. (2022 October). *Foodbank Hunger Report 2022,* Foodbank.org.au

5. Muir, K., Carey, G., Weier, M., Brown, G., Barraket, J., Qian, J. & Flatau, P. (n.d.). *Building Back Better: Pulse of the For-Purpose Sector,* Centre for Social Impact.

6. benefolk.org. (n.d.). *Reset 2020 - Benefolk | Social Impact Specialist Community.* [online] Available at: https://benefolk.org/reset-2020 [Accessed 27 Nov. 2023].

7. *Corporate partnership with $73M impact that's democratising contemporary art.* [online] www.artshub.com.au. Available at: https://www.artshub.com.au/news/news/corporate-partnership-with-73m-impact-thats-democratising-contemporary-art-2493368/ [Accessed 27 Nov. 2023].

8. *2022 Edelman Trust Barometer.* [online] Edelman. Available at: https://www.edelman.com/trust/2022-trust-barometer.

9. Beyond Blue (2022). *Learn about mental health - Beyond Blue.* [online] www.beyondblue.org.au. Available at: https://www.beyondblue.org.au/mental-health.

10. auspost.com.au. (n.d.). *Mental health.* [online] Available at: https://auspost.com.au/about-us/supporting-communities/mental-health. [Accessed 27 Nov. 2023].

CHAPTER 2

1. McLeod, J. (2022). *Corporate Support Report - JBWere.* [online] www.jbwere.com.au. Available at: https://www.jbwere.com.au/campaigns/corporate-support-report [Accessed 27 Nov. 2023].

2. Paul, M. (2020). *Impact of COVID-19 On Fundraising July 2020.* [online] More Strategic. Available at: https://morestrategic.com.au/impact-of-covid-19-on-fundraising-july-2020/ [Accessed 27 Nov. 2023].

3. Forensics today PwC perspectives on the newest risks drawing investigator scrutiny. (April 2023). Available at: https://www.pwc.com/us/en/services/consulting/cybersecurity-risk-regulatory/assets/pwc-cyber-forensics-today-esg-in-gov-pdf-v2.pdf [Accessed 27 Nov. 2023].

4. Edelman (2023). *2023 Edelman Trust Barometer.* [online] Edelman. Available at: https://www.edelman.com/trust/2023/trust-barometer.

5. Yellow (2022). *Yellow Pages partnership with mental health advocacy group R U OK?* [online] Yellow Pages. Available at: https://www.yellow.com.au/partnerships/ruok/.

6. Cain, A. (2021). *Technology a lifesaver for Lifeline.* [online] The Sydney Morning Herald. Available at: https://www.smh.com.au/technology/technology-a-lifesaver-for-lifeline-20211011-p58z0e.html [Accessed 27 Nov. 2023].

7. Bailey, I. (2021). *Target pledges $250,000 to support vulnerable mothers and children - Ragtrader.* [online] www.ragtrader.com.au.

Available at: https://www.ragtrader.com.au/news/target-pledges-250-000-to-support-vulnerable-mothers-and-children [Accessed 27 Nov. 2023].

8. Centre for Social Impact, (2019). *Three to tango: achieving marriage equality in Australia.* [online] Available at www.csi.edu.au/research

9. www.reckitt.com. (2015). *RB and Save the Children launch groundbreaking partnership to reduce child deaths from diarrhoea – RB.* [online] Available at: https://reckitt.com/us/newsroom/latest-news/news/2015/march/rb-and-save-the-children-launch-groundbreaking-partnership-to-reduce-child-deaths-from-diarrhoea [Accessed 27 Nov. 2023].

10. Jabr, F. (2021). *A vast, ancient and intricate society: the secret social network of old-growth forests.* [online] The Sydney Morning Herald. Available at: https://www.smh.com.au/environment/sustainability/a-vast-ancient-and-intricate-society-the-secret-social-network-of-old-growth-forests-20200703-p558ti.html [Accessed 27 Nov. 2023].

11. Global Justice Now (2018). *69 of the Richest 100 Entities on the Planet Are corporations, Not governments, Figures Show.* [online] Global Justice. Available at: https://www.globaljustice.org.uk/news/69-richest-100-entities-planet-are-corporations-not-governments-figures-show/.

12. Mendoza, K.A. (2021). *iTWire - Fujitsu and Camp Quality develop an app that informs kids about cancer.* [online] itwire.com. Available at: https://itwire.com/it-people-news/education/fujitsu-and-camp-quality-develop-an-app-that-informs-kids-about-cancer.html [Accessed 27 Nov. 2023].

CHAPTER 3

1. tiltify.com. (2018). *Tiltify - Made for Fundraisers.* [online] Available at: https://tiltify.com/save-the-children/2022-survive-to-5 [Accessed 27 Nov. 2023].

2. Garvan Institute, (2018). *DreamLab delivers a new way to make sense of cancer | Garvan Institute of Medical Research.* [online]

www.garvan.org.au. Available at: https://www.garvan.org.au/news-resources/news/dreamlab-delivers-a-new-way-to-make-sense-of-cancer [Accessed 27 Nov. 2023].

3. Welch, K. (2022). *Hanes, Coles and Special Group tell Australians to 'Take on Cancer in Your Undies' in support of Ovarian Cancer.* [online] Mumbrella. Available at: https://mumbrella.com.au/hanes-coles-and-special-group-tell-australians-to-take-on-cancer-in-your-undies-in-support-of-ovarian-cancer-733603 [Accessed 27 Nov. 2023].

4. Save the Children's Resource Centre. (2018). *The Dirty Truth about the Infant Formula Industry.* [online] Available at: https://resourcecentre.savethechildren.net/document/dirty-truth-about-infant-formula-industry/ [Accessed 27 Nov. 2023].

5. Canas, S. (2023). *Boot the Blues webinar 2023.* [online] Steel Blue. Available at: https://steelblue.com/au/boot-the-blues-webinar-2023-steel-blue/ [Accessed 27 Nov. 2023].

6. NSW State Emergency Service. (2023). *Partnerships.* [online] Available at: https://www.ses.nsw.gov.au/about-us/partnerships [Accessed 27 Nov. 2023].

7. Sas, N. (2022). 'Crying crocodile tears': The impact of Airbnb as Australia's rental crisis bites. *ABC News.* [online] 28 Dec. Available at: https://www.abc.net.au/news/2022-12-29/influence-of-air-bnb-on-australian-rental-crisis/101809556.

8. Daley, P. (2020). The strange case of the weapons maker and the Australian children's charity. *The Guardian.* [online] 4 Dec. Available at: https://www.theguardian.com/commentisfree/2020/dec/04/the-strange-case-of-the-weapons-maker-and-the-australian-childrens-charity.

9. Our Ethical Charter. (2023). Available at: https://www.mardigras.org.au/wp-content/uploads/2022/03/sglmg-2021-ethical-charter.pdf.

10. Australian Ballet. (2021). *Our pas de deux with Chanel.* [online] Available at: https://australianballet.com.au/blog/our-pas-de-deux-with-chanel.

CHAPTER 4

1. Gilbert, E. (2016). *Big Magic*. Penguin USA.

2. Vegemite (2023), www.vegemite.com.au

3. BHP (2023). *Annual report 2023*. [online] Bhp.com. Available at: https://www.bhp.com/investors/annual-reporting/annual-report-2023.

4. Save the Children UK. (2023). *Christmas Jumper Day 2023*. [online] Available at: https://www.savethechildren.org.uk/christmas-jumper-day [Accessed 27 Nov. 2023].

5. Col Fink. (2023). *Col Fink*. [online] Available at: https://www.colfink.com/ [Accessed 27 Nov. 2023].

6. www.legacy.com.au. (2023). *Centenary – Legacy*. [online] Available at: https://www.legacy.com.au/centenary/ [Accessed 27 Nov. 2023].

CHAPTER 5

1. Gallo, A. (2022). *The value of keeping the right customers*. [online] Harvard Business Review. Available at: https://hbr.org/2014/10/the-value-of-keeping-the-right-customers.

2. Holmes, H. (2022). *Tesco and WWF: a 'ground-breaking' partnership?* [online] The Grocer. Available at: https://www.thegrocer.co.uk/tesco/tesco-and-wwf-a-ground-breaking-partnership/664936.article.

3. Kantaria, P. (2019). *Macmillan's partnership with Boots named 'most admired' corporate partnership*. [online] www.civilsociety.co.uk. Available at: https://www.civilsociety.co.uk/news/macmillan-s-partnership-with-boots-wins-the-most-admired-corporate-partnership.html.

4. GlaxoSmithKline (2019). *GSK and Save the Children partnership Working together to help save one million children's lives*. [online] Available at: https://www.gsk.com/media/5379/save-the-children-partnership-brochure.pdf.

CHAPTER 6

1. Tough Mudder Australia. (2023). *Tough Mudder Australia Mud Run*. [online] Available at: https://toughmudder.com.au/.

CHAPTER 7

1. Handy, C. (2015). *The Second Curve: Thoughts on Reinventing Society*. Penguin Random House.

2. Race, M. & Hooker, L. (2022). Ukraine conflict: Growing numbers of firms pull back from Russia. *BBC News*. [online] 3 Mar. Available at: https://www.bbc.com/news/business-60571133.

3. Deloitte (2014). *Big demands and high expectations The Deloitte Millennial Survey Executive summary*. [online] Available at: https://www2.deloitte.com/content/dam/Deloitte/global/Documents/About-Deloitte/gx-dttl-2014-millennial-survey-report.pdf.

4. ACCP (2023). *4th ANNUAL CSR INSIGHTS SURVEY*. [online] Association of Corporate Citizenship Professionals. Available at: https://accp.org/resources/csr-resources/4th-annual-csr-insights-survey/ [Accessed 27 Nov. 2023].

5. Blackbaud (2023). *Blackbaud Releases 11th Annual Industry Report on Corporate Social Responsibility and Employee Engagement Trends*. [online] Blackbaud. Available at: https://www.blackbaud.com/newsroom/article/blackbaud-releases-11th-annual-industry-report-on-corporate-social-responsibility-and-employee-engagement-trends [Accessed 27 Nov. 2023].

6. Hari, J. (2022). *Stolen Focus*. Bloomsbury Publishing Ltd.

7. Australia Post (2023). *When PostPride joined Beyond Blue in the Mardi Gras Parade*. [online] auspost.com.au. Available at: https://auspost.com.au/community-hub/mental-health-wellbeing/mardi-gras-australia-post-beyond-blue [Accessed 27 Nov. 2023].

Acknowledgments

We always say that partnerships need the whole village to be successful and this book is the perfect example. We are truly grateful for the support and inspiration from many people to get this book finished.

Thanks to Kelly Irving and your amazing community at the Expert Author Academy for providing the expertise, structure and insights to build a coherent book from a scrappy first draft. Our gratitude to Jenny Magee for her eagle eyes in editing and Sylvie Blair for demystifying the tricky world of book publishing.

Sincere thanks to the advance readers who read and reviewed our book. We are very touched by your kindness, suggestions and encouragement.

We are inspired by Julia Keady at Benefolk, who has built a community of people that are leading the way on collaboration. Not only does she have a vision for raising the capability and wellbeing of the non-profit sector, but she actually gets stuff done.

Thanks to the mentors, faculty and fellow travellers in the Thought Leaders business community. The generosity of this community is overwhelming and it's inspiring to be in your company. A very special thanks to Monique Richardson who threw down the gauntlet of a tight deadline to finish the book and reignited our determination.

We continue to be encouraged and inspired by our many non-profit clients striving to make the world a better place. Special recognition to the partnership executives, who are the most talented, versatile, creative and savvy bunch of people in the universe. To all of you dealing with shoestring budgets, difficult clients and misguided bosses but still trying to succeed. In particular, the partnership executive working solo in a small organisation with little support and no budget to access training courses or conferences — you're the real inspiration for the book.

The CSR, ESG, community managers and corporate foundation heads who are re-thinking how business operates and trying to make a real impact. Thank you for your commitment to meaningful partnerships.

We remember the corporate and NFP bosses who taught us so much- good and bad. You helped build our knowledge and kindled the fire to do better.

We dedicate this book to our families — Ruby, Richard, Thomas and Isabelle. Our hope is to leave a better world for them.

Let's Work Out
What You Need

Book a Free Chat here:

Contact details:

W   stellarpartnerships.com

E   info@stellarpartnerships.com

P   0414 640 602